BLUFF YOUR WAY IN LITERATURE

MICHAEL KERRIGAN

RAVETTE BOOKS

John Godfrey
from '93

Published by Ravette Books Limited
3 Glenside Estate, Star Road,
Partridge Green, Horsham,
West Sussex RH13 8RA
(0403) 710392

First printed 1987
Revised 1991

Series Editor – Anne Tauté

Cover design – Jim Wire
Typesetting – Input Typesetting Ltd.
Printing and binding – Cox & Wyman Ltd.
Production – Oval Projects Ltd.

The Bluffer's Guides are based on
an original idea by Peter Wolfe.

CONTENTS

INTRODUCTION

Bluffing your way in literature is made a lot easier by the fact that everybody else, however knowledgeable, is doing it too, and there is really nothing else you can do. It's far too big a field for any one person to master, and it gets bigger each week as new books follow old in an unending, uncontainable torrent.

In the meantime, the literary world is still awaiting (with qualified eagerness) a half-way serviceable definition of the word 'literature' itself. When that day comes, various interesting questions (such as 'How do we know whether a work is any good?', 'What counts as literature and what doesn't?', 'What is literary criticism?') will be answered. The fact that we literally don't know what we're talking about has not, of course, been enough to quell the indomitable spirit of the literary community – so you certainly shouldn't let it stand in your way.

Since recent attempts to define terms more rigorously have succeeded only in making an answer look further away than ever, and in casting doubt over the very existence of 'literature', we're left to make do with older assumptions (which actually do the job admirably). Victorian schools inspector Matthew Arnold thought literature was 'the best that is known and thought in the world', and was rash enough to say so. In fact, while Arnold has been churlishly taken to task over the meaninglessness of this statement, it's his definition that we all use, though we go to more or less elaborate lengths to conceal it.

We know what 'the best' is because the literary community – a loose assemblage of academics, journalists and publishers, tell us. 'Literary criticism' is just the way they tell it.

As will become clear once you've practised for a

while, the elusiveness that makes literary criticism seem so forbidding is actually your greatest asset. The very woolliness of the discipline facilitates the instant redefining of terms and general goalpost-moving that will keep you out of trouble. Providing you exercise reasonable care in avoiding statements on matters of incontrovertible fact (and you'll be surprised how few of those there are), there is really no reason ever to be caught in the wrong. Literary texts are infinitely complex; with one thing always symbolizing another, one meaning forever being undercut by another level of irony, so as long as you're prepared to stand firm there's no real chance of your interpretation being proved incorrect.

Of secondary importance, a nodding acquaintance with some of the Greats of literature will undoubtedly come in handy from time to time, and succeeding sections of this guide will do their best to bring you together. It is not their intention to foster real intimacy between yourself and these giants. Serious devotion to literature may conflict with your first loyalty, which should always be to bluffing.

THE LITERARY COMMUNITY

The literary community divides broadly into two main sections, Academics and Media. Some ingenuous souls would argue that there is also a third section, the writers themselves, but in practice, apart from providing some of your conversational raw material, they're of pretty negligible importance.

Novelists and poets can play an active role only if they've succeeded in winning a place in one of these two sections: in the academy as teachers or objects of study, and in the media as 'personalities' or reviewers. The writers themselves have increasingly to be able to bluff about their own work either to justify it in terms 'serious' enough to warrant the attention of the academics, or to reduce it to a few epigrams and anecdotes suitable for easy absorption by the newspaper reader or television audience. The mark of true genius, of course, is the ability to do both at once.

The Academics

If you are currently undergoing education and thus in daily contact with teachers of literature, you can be forgiven for thinking that this section actually is the literary community – particularly since academics, who half believe this themselves, are unlikely to do anything to discourage the impression. This is a misapprehension. Ranging from the humblest schoolteacher to the most exalted professor, the academics may be the largest section of the literary community numerically, but as opinion-formers they are nothing like as important as they like to think.

This is in part because the academic world has no

strong collective identity. It is riven by bitter and deep-rooted political disputes. There is little common ground between the ultra-conservative element (staunch custodians of 'standards' and protectors of the 'canon', and tireless spotters of the split-infinitive, and the present generation who regard correct spelling as an instrument of oppression. Distrust and disunity are endemic in an environment where individuals get ahead largely by doing down each other's work.

Most of its denizens are too ground down by crippling teaching and administrative loads and productivity targets to give too much attention to literature. Academic critics have long been rendered marginal to the main currents of literary discussion by the extreme specialization and dryness of their work.

Demoralized they may be, but academics are by no means entirely without influence so it would be a mistake to dismiss them too lightly. While there is very little academic criticism you need know about and none you have to read, the academic world is the only institutionalized structure capable of giving novelists and poets the sort of 'official' recognition they crave.

The Media

The few academics who do manage to make a significant individual mark on the literary scene do so because they've succeeded in crossing over and establishing themselves as recognizable figures in the media.

In the review pages of the quality press, specialized literary journals, and on radio and television, the big decisions are made as to what really matters and what can be safely ignored. Here the decision-makers are a motley crew of full-time journalists, moonlighting 'real' writers and a host of hacks for whom anything, even book reviewing, is preferable to honest work.

You don't really have to read books at all to get by as a literary bluffer. To dip into reviews is a good deal more time-efficient than reading the books themselves (which in any case merely tend to confuse the issue).

Apart from the national daily and weekend papers, which review much the same books in much the same terms, if you scan a selection of mainstream journals regularly you won't go too far wrong. There are in addition, scores of smaller publications catering for special interests. It does the bluffer no harm to have a clearly personalized perspective on things.

(Im) Postures

Bluffing in literature – like bluffing in any other area – can be as much about applied anthropology as knowledge of the field. Decide what sort of image you want to project and stick to it. Complete, unqualified self-assurance is the key to bluffing success, but it's easier to achieve this if you have an image (or persona) you can relax and be uninhibitedly fraudulent in.

There are many acceptable images for the bluffer: Tortured Artist, Sensitive Aesthete, European Intellectual, etc. As you grow more confident you will probably want to experiment with refinements and new permutations.

Specialized positions help cut down the workload too, for bluffing can be as much a matter of what you don't know as what you do. For the European Intellectual, for instance, a contemptuous ignorance of English writing is not so much permissible as mandatory. The

Sensitive Aesthete, on the other hand, is free to remain loftily unaware of even the most important continental heavyweights but must compensate with a knowledge of, and outward enthusiasm for, some fairly dire Victorian verse.

Two extreme roles in particular offer beginners credible ways of cutting down the workload.

1. The Cultural Materialist

This pose awes bourgeoise opponents, making them feel guilty and deferential. Though literature is important to you in principle, you're deeply suspicious of it. Critical Theory, especially when it's Marxist, gives you ways of blowing the lid off the great 'culture' swindle.

The great virtue of this pose is that it is the only one in which being caught out in ignorance of some classic work of literature not only does not work against you, but even counts in your favour. The savings in labour are considerable. However you do have to earn your place at the literary table with some command of theory.

2. The Fogey

In this guise, most of your pretended reading is in the Greek and Latin classics, ecclesiastical history and obscure devotional poetry of the eighteenth and nineteenth centuries. Twentieth century literature, which you will claim for the most part to be a regrettable mistake, is dominated by the towering figures of Belloc and Chesterton, but A.N. Wilson and Barbara Pym also show some merit. Your books are by and large antiquarian first editions, and criticism is for you the 'enemy of literature'.

This pose has the immense advantages of being the one really foolproof way of avoiding difficult Critical Theory. On the other hand, the necessity of reading *The Spectator* with apparent enjoyment and looking like someone who's studied St. John Chrysostom in the original Greek could well make the price seem too high.

Whatever the benefits, the effort involved in maintaining either of these roles effectively can be considerable, and most bluffers will find it easier in the long run to persevere in some more easy-going, middle-of-the-road eclecticism. These are merely offered as last resorts, in case the strain of appearing informed on either great classics or abstruse theories proves too great.

BRITAIN

The Novel

The 'birth of the Novel' took place at some point during the early eighteenth century, but its exact date of birth and parentage are hotly disputed. The two defendants in the paternity suit are **Daniel Defoe** (with *Robinson Crusoe*, 1719) and **Samuel Richardson** (*Pamela*, 1740).

To complicate matters still further, Dale Spender has put forward a hundred 'Mothers of the Novel', including many who, like **Aphra Behn** (1640-89) and **Delariviere Manley** (1663-1724), got there well before either 'Father'. The fact is that prose fiction (romances and 'memoirs') had been going for years, and nobody can explain what makes the 'new' novel stand out in this crowd. So you can safely choose your own parent — the more obscure the better — without much fear of contradiction.

Father or not, Richardson is *the* early novelist to be seen with at the moment. *Pamela* and the later *Clarissa*, both formerly regarded as moralizing, naive and highly tedious, have rocketed to the top of the league. *Clarissa* may be the longest novel in the English language, but you "couldn't put it down". It's very boring to find it boring. *Tom Jones*, by **Henry Fielding** (1707-54) — long the undisputed champion — trails a long way behind, its robust, manly humour now a bit of an embarrassment.

With such a confused family background, it was inevitable that the young novel would go off the rails — which it did in spectacular style in the 1760s, with **Laurence Sterne** and his *Tristram Shandy*, a riot of literary and typographical jokes without detectable plot. You should, like it or not, accept its importance as a "remarkable exploration of the practice of writing", though you can always score points by noting that none of Sterne's tricks were in themselves new. At about the same time, the crazy, mixed-up genre started showing signs of further instability with the **Gothic Novel**, literally dreamed up by **Horace Walpole**, whose *The Castle of Otranto* (1760) was soon eclipsed by a spate of melodramatic and improbably-plotted chillers, culminating at the end of the century in the works of **Anne Radcliffe**, author of the smash-hit *Mysteries of Udolpho*. Contempt for the Gothic House of Horror isn't allowed. Ironic approval is OK — better still, say you admire its "frank engagement with Unreason".

Mary Wollstonecraft (1759-97), though primarily a feminist thinker, has recently become a highly respected 'novelist' despite never having completed a 'novel' above short story length. A real gift for the bluffer, then, given the monstrous size of many of the other eighteenth century classics. Neither **Fanny Burney** (1752-1840) nor **Maria Edgeworth** (1767-1849) suffered from this kind of writing block, each producing respectable numbers of hefty volumes. Edgeworth had the revolutionary idea that people might be interested in reading about life in the provinces, and thus pioneered the 'regional novel', carving out for herself a footnote in literary history. Now, however, she is seen as sharing with Burney the even more revolutionary idea that you could have a heroine who wasn't a complete idiot, and who didn't get abducted, drugged, raped, etc. in the course of the novel. Their social comedies on the more everyday perils of the heroine facing adulthood and the marriage market opened the way for **Jane Austen** (1775-1817).

Reports of **Sir Walter Scott**'s comeback are, as usual, greatly exaggerated. Despite promising material — passion and blood-feud in the wilds of Scotland — the going is slow (Scott's "relentless exposure of the historical process") and bodices remain disappointingly unripped.

His influence in Europe was enormous, if undeserved. (You cherish your recording of Callas in *Lucia di Lammermoor*). After Scott, the next novelist of note was **Charles Dickens**, who published his first novel, *The Pickwick Papers*, in 1836, and died in the middle of his fourteenth, *The Mystery of Edwin Drood*, thirty-four years and several whopping royalty cheques later. His early novels are easily spotted — they all have grotesque characters, mawkish deathbed scenes and a tendency to be televised on Sunday afternoons. The "brooding intensity" of his last novels, however, makes them "Dostoyevskyan" and hence useful bluffing material. The novels of Dickens' successor, **William Makepeace Thackeray are** throw backs to the eighteenth century, though the later ones make concessions to their time in the form of some quite nauseating sentimentality. *Vanity Fair* (1848), however, packs a nasty, cynical punch that none of the other Victorian novels even approaches. And after a long period out in the cold, Thackeray seems to be clawing his way back into fashion. The **Brontë** sisters, **Charlotte** (1816-55), **Emily** (1818-48), and **Anne** (1820-49), wrote highly original — and wildly romantic — novels which didn't fit easily into any obvious tradition in the nineteenth century. They do now, though. Emily's moody, violent Heathcliff and Charlotte's mousy heroines are the earliest recognizable prototypes for today's Mills and Boon/Harlequin romances.

Every once in a while, some hapless bluffer blithely joins in a conversation on **George Eliot** (1819-80) without having grasped the simple but nonetheless crucial fact that she was a woman and that her real name was Mary Ann Evans. The inevitable result is crushing humiliation. George Eliot is the high priestess of 'mature' (not to be confused with 'adult') fiction. This means that her novels are full of complex interactions between complex

14

characters, and thus rather heavy going — though you mustn't say so. **Thomas Hardy** (1840-1928) is most famous as a novelist, but be sure to agree with his own view that he was much better as a poet. His novels, set in rural 'Wessex' were never a bundle of laughs but they got more and more gloomy as they went on, until by the time of the late ones like *Tess of the d'Urbervilles* (1891) and *Jude the Obscure* (1896), Hardy's unrelenting pessimism provides comic relief all by itself.

Born in 1857, in Poland, Teodor Jósef Konrad Nalecz Korzeniowski, or **Joseph Conrad,** had a somewhat unlikely background for a great twentieth-century English novelist, but there it is. After twenty years' seafaring, he settled in England to write — often about the sea, always about the dark forces of anarchy within civilized man (good phrase). Though he lived until 1970, **E. M. Forster** got all his novels out of the way in the first twenty years of the century, after which he settled down in Cambridge to become a famous man of letters (males who can pass for over forty should always refer to him as 'Morgan' and say that they "knew him at Kings"). Why his thoroughly conventional novels and wishy-washy liberal views should make Forster a 'major novelist' isn't clear. But you can't avoid him — especially now he's become a successful screenwriter.

Don't even think about liking **D. H. Lawrence** (1885-1930). The steady detumescence of his reputation continues, and there are no signs of the lambent flame being rekindled. Revered as late as the sixties, 'the great sexual liberator and scourge of bourgeois values', 'the first man to understand women's sexuality', simply aren't recognizable in the ranting, authoritarian misogynist Lawrence looks like today.

Virginia Woolf (1882-1941) perfected the 'stream of consciousness' novel, in which the reader is subjected to the unconnected thoughts of (usually neurotic) characters without any protection from the author. Or, indeed, much in the way of action. If this technique really does show how people's minds work, it explains a lot about the state of the world. Stream of consciousness is just one of the dozens of devices used by **James Joyce** (also 1882-1941) in his extremely elaborate *Ulysses* and quite unreadable *Finnegans Wake*. Learn the last five lines of the former, and maintain stoutly that the latter is your favourite bedtime reading. Few will dare to call your bluff.

Poetry

The oldest surviving British poetry dates from the seventh century, but it's in Anglo-Saxon and understood only by a handful of academics. A knowledge of Anglo-Saxon poetry is unlikely to make you the life and soul of the party and it's best left well alone. Nothing of which the bluffer need take any notice happened until the second half of the fourteenth century with the works of **Geoffrey Chaucer**. A civil servant, Chaucer wrote his poems in his spare time (though not, as far as we know, in triplicate). You should prefer his long poem of tragic passion, *Troilus and Criseyde* but also, of course, love the more famous *Canterbury Tales*. This brilliant, and in the main entertaining, collection of stories told by a group of pilgrims on the road was originally intended to be four times as long as it is, each pilgrim telling two tales on the way out to Canterbury and two on the way back. Unfortunately Chaucer never got past the first round — presumably bored into a stupor by the stultifying *Parson's Tale* during which the work breaks off. You should be aware of the existence of Chaucer's approximate contemporaries, **William Langland** (author of the religious poem *The Vision of Piers Plowman*) and the anonymous writer of the chivalous romance *Sir Gawain and the Green Knight* — known, appropriately enough, as **The Gawain Poet**. Beyond that, and a conviction that both are absurdly underrated, you don't need to know anything else.

After this period, the next poetic wave of any importance comes in the late fifteenth and early sixteenth centuries, with the Scottish poets **Robert Henryson**, **Gavin Douglas** and **William Dunbar**. They are of most interest to the Scottish bluffer, who can make a lot of mileage out of indignantly rejecting the label 'Scots Chaucerians' traditionally applied to the trio.

Things started hotting up as the sixteenth century went on, with the advent of **Sir Thomas Wyatt** (1503-42) — courtier, supposed boyfriend of Anne Boleyn and author of lugubrious love lyrics, as well as the less familiar satires, which the smart bluffer will affect to prefer. Wyatt's younger contemporary, **Surrey** (strictly speaking Henry Howard, Earl of Surrey) was long considered superior. But his smooth, more polished style is now disdained as lacking Wyatt's 'ruggedness'. Between the two of them, Wyatt and Surrey popularized the Sonnet form in England, and for the next half-century poets struggled manfully — if not always very effectively — to cram their loftiest sentiments into fourteen-line moulds. Some did succeed, notably **Sir Philip Sidney** (1554-86). It is decidedly not on to say that his *Astrophel and Stella* collection is too clever by half. Like the works of the other sonneteers, it is not a love story but an "experiment in form", an "investigation into the nature of language". It is also a *sequence* — i.e. you're supposed to plough through all 108 sonnets at one go. Far too many of the early sonneteers were addicted to this barbarous practice. **William Shakespeare**'s sonnets make life even more difficult: no one can agree what order they're supposed to go in, and they're addressed to two different people, a fair young man and a 'dark lady'. Arguments about who these characters were tend to get very heated, fantastically complicated, and end in tears (or wild claims that Shakepeare was really married to the Man Right Fair). Don't get involved.

Although **Edmund Spenser** wrote some rather dreary sonnets (the *Amoretti*), these are the least of your worries. His most famous work is the *Faerie Queene*, a long and extremely tiresome romance in which chivalrous knights representing the different Virtues slog it out with foul monsters (you've guessed it, the Vices). Thankfully, Spenser never completed this already enormous poem, and some of what he *did* finish was wasted when Irish rebels burned down his peasant-bashing patron's castle — an early example of practical criticism for which all bluffers should be grateful.

John Donne (1572-1631) wrote raffish, but often remarkably intense love lyrics, as well as intense, but often remarkably raffish religious poetry. His style is rough and dramatic rather than even and soothing, and he has a liking for ingenious and far-fetched images ('conceits'). These qualities make him the figurehead for the 'Metaphysical Poets' — not a real group or movement, but heterogeneous poets yoked together by violence in later criticism. The most important Metaphysicals, including the religious poets **George Herbert** (1593-1633) and **Henry Vaughan** (1622-95), share some of Donne's characteristics, but are on the whole much less anxious to shock.

John Milton (1608-74), a sort of official pamphleteer for Oliver Cromwell's government, decided that the new and glorious liberated England needed its own protestant national epic. Unfortunately, before he could get round to writing it, the Stuarts had been restored and England was the same old king-ridden country it had always been. Milton retired to the country in disgust and wrote *Paradise Lost*, about the fall of Adam and Eve and their expulsion from Eden. Impressive stuff, but as Dr. Johnson later remarked, 'None ever wished it longer than it is'. Milton's assistant as Cromwellian Saatchi and Saatchi was **Andrew Marvell** (1621-78). A man of great poetic — and political — versatility, Marvell had been a royalist before the troubles, and had written in a broadly metaphysical, style. Always an enemy of bigotry, however, he quickly adjusted, doing his best to support (and make a living from) the new régime. With the Restoration, Marvell again became an instant royalist (just add state pension) and started writing political satires.

As if to confirm the Puritans' worst fears, Charles II had hardly unpacked his Duty Free when his courtiers started churning out 'Restoration Poetry'. Notorious freethinker and sex maniac **John Wilmot, Earl of Rochester** became the undisputed *doyen* of lavatory-wall literature. Don't be fooled by admirers of his 'more philosophical late poetry' — their copies always fall open at the wrong page. Less flamboyant, less aristocratic, but much more 'important' than Rochester, **John Dryden** (1631-1700), though a successful dramatist, is now admired more for his straight poetry. Dryden rashly took on such thankless tasks as putting forward the positive sides of the Fire of London and the humiliating Dutch War of 1666 (in *Annus Mirabilis*), lending money to Charles II, and converting to Catholicism just before the accession of William of Orange. His *MacFlecknoe* (a literary exocet fired at a pushy rival) was, like the rest of his poetry, much respected by the **Augustans**.

Despite their admiration for the Age of Augustus (31 BC - AD 14) and its classic, balanced poetry (Virgil, Horace, Ovid) the Augustans (c.1700-1750) showed a deplorably modern taste in unbalanced, mud-slinging attacks, many of them on **Alexander Pope** (1688-1744), Catholic, 4'6" and hunchbacked from childhood. Pope's *Dunciad* (which takes up where *MacFlecknoe* left off) wiped the floor with all comers; its spoof footnotes and index "anticipate *The Waste Land*" (and/or *Finnegans Wake*) into the bargain. The curse of the *Dunciad* was fulfilled; the only other Augustan poets you need know about now are Pope's friends **Gay** and **Swift**, though the one is more famous for *The Beggars' Opera* and the other for his *Gulliver's Travels*. Praise Gay's streetwise London poem, *Trivia*. **Samuel (Dr.) Johnson** brought up the Augustan rear in the mid-century, but produced only two 'important' poems, both cribbed from Juvenal.

Though *Jerusalem* is beloved of Women's Institutes and School Governors, they'd have looked askance at its author, **William Blake** (1757-1827), all-round anarchist and advocate of free love, given to nude games of 'Paradise Lost' with his wife in the back garden. Blakeolatry boomed (predictably) in the sixties, and fans have calmed down since. He's still important, though, for his own work, and as a proto-Romantic. **Romanticism** begins in 1798 (one of the few Dates in literary history) with *Lyrical Ballads* by **William Wordsworth** and **Samuel Taylor Coleridge** — or rather, with its *Preface*. It claims that the Poet (Romantics *adore* capital letters) is 'a man speaking to men' — just more sensitive, intelligent, 'comprehensive-souled', etc. than other men. The poems (always second fiddle in Romantic collections) don't deliver the goods. Wordsworth's later *Prelude* (an early version of Sinatra's 'My Way') describes the development of his own 'comprehensive soul' in exhaustive detail. N.B. Wordsworth also invented the Lake District.

Percy Bysshe Shelley (silliest middle name in literature?) also wrote great prefaces as well as some important poems, mostly on the popular Romantic theme of the individual's struggle against impersonal conventions. His short lyrics, though streets ahead of his long poems and verse dramas, aren't as 'important'. Shelley's best-known long poem, *Adonais* (1821), commemorates **John Keats**' death from TB that year, aged 26. Keats wrote his prefaces in his letters, which must have been fun for his friends. His most important poems are the *Odes*, in which he pontificates about Life, Death and Art to various hapless Nightingales, Grecian Urns, etc.

The most romantic Romantic was **George Gordon, Lord Byron** (1788-1824), a nineteenth-century Rochester, whose affairs (especially that with half-sister Augusta) pleasantly scandalized the nation. His early sizzlers about dashing, desperate outlaws were hugely popular, but his *Don Juan*, mixing melodrama with unRomantic scepticism and wit, is more attractive nowadays.

Alfred Lord Tennyson (1809-92), once the most popular Victorian poet, is still admired for his technical virtuosity, though his sentimentalism and shallow philosophizing deter most modern readers. Back his *In Memoriam* rather than the kitschy *Idylls of the King*. He is nevertheless a sight better than **Matthew Arnold** (1822-88), who produced the most luxuriant sidewhiskers and arguably the dreariest poetry of his era. Arnold is still 'important', though, for expressing (however badly) the latter's 'central preoccupations'. Ignoring Victorian hobbyhorses, **Robert Browning** (1812-89) wrote sophisticated, witty (often impenetrable) 'dramatic monologues': chatty exposés of bizarre individuals under stress. **Gerard Manley Hopkins, SJ** (1844-89) is even less penetrable than Browning. It takes a Jesuit to think up something as perverse as 'sprung rhythm' — literally 'offbeat' poetry, littered with accents and hyphens. Forget *Pied Beauty*, etc. — go for the *Terrible* (sic) *Sonnets*.

If you must like any of the (First World) **War Poets**, make it the adventurous and sophisticated **Isaac Rosenberg**, a "neglected Modernist". The others, like **Wilfred Owen**, **Siegfried Sassoon**, etc., are strictly teen reading. Between occult lore, Irish myths and politics, **W. B. Yeats** (1865-1939) is heavy going. However he's indispensable, and a nodding acquaintance with the *Lake Isle of Innisfree* won't do. Affect to like the more abstract *Last Poems* — supposedly the toughest, though there's not much in it.

Thomas Stearns Eliot (1888-1965), not to be confused with George (see The Novel), a bank clerk from St. Louis, Missouri, became a Great English Poet with *The Waste Land* and some help from Ezra Pound, who didn't (see Americans). Point out that his Sanskrit is kindergarten standard, and don't be fooled by the *Notes*. If in doubt, prefer the complex and 'serious' *Four Quartets*. **Wystan Hugh Auden** (silliest first name in English Literature?) emigrated to America (in 1939) but didn't become a Great American Poet. The 'English Auden' was a left-wing intellectual who wrote powerful (but unponderous) poems. The 'American Auden' got religion and drink, and it was downhill all the way.

Drama

Drama is usually discussed as 'theatre' ('sensitive use of scaffolding in Act Three'; 'X's *marvellous* Lear', etc.)

rather than as 'literature'. Theatrical bluffing is a specialized discipline with values and vocabulary all its own. (See *The Bluffer's Guide to Theatre* for details.) Some drama does fall within the domain of 'literature', though, and you might have to talk about it in those terms. As a general rule, anything written (however badly) before 1700 counts as 'literature' as well as 'theatre', while anything written (however well) after this is just 'theatre'.

British drama is thought by scholars to have grown out of the Catholic Mass — strong on props and costumes, but a bit short on action. After a continuous run of several centuries, the burghers of England's medieval towns decided that something extra was needed. Thus the **Mystery Plays** were developed. Nothing to do with *The Mousetrap* or *The Name of the Rose*, Mystery Plays were thoroughly unmysterious run-throughs of the well-loved Bible stories. If you'd already read the book and knew the ending ('It was Pontius Pilate'), you could try a **Morality Play**. These tended to start off well, with amiable characters like Lust, Envy, Gluttony and Sloth, but the moral majority, as usual, ended up hogging the microphone. Mysteries and Moralities alike were suppressed by the Puritans of the sixteenth century, on the somewhat unlikely grounds that they were too much fun.

Medieval dramas had normally been collective efforts, early 'Community Theatre'; the first known 'Great Dramatists' cropped up in the Elizabethan England of the 1590s. **Christopher Marlowe** (1564-93), notorious atheist and secret agent, was also the author of several major tragedies, which you can say "link the morality tradition with the modern theatre". His most important play remains *Doctor Faustus*, but be sure to mention the up-and-coming *Jew of Malta*. After Marlowe comes the bard himself, **William Shakespeare** (1564-1616), still regarded as the greatest English writer of all time and, by the English themselves, as the greatest in the history of the World. Shakespeare is a thorn in the flesh for all bluffers. He produced a lot of writing (about 37 plays' worth) and it's all supposed to run in your veins. The relevant sections in Dictionaries of Quotations can sometimes help in giving the juiciest bits at a glance, but usually, compiled in more sentimental times, they ignore the really impressive, intellectual passages, and favour the less useful 'Hey, ho, the wind and the rain' -type bits. It's probably best to get to know a couple of plays (see them in controversial productions, killing two birds with one stone, and learn a handful of quotes), then grapple them to your soul with hoops of steel, producing them at every available opportunity.

Remember that there is no *one*, 'official' version of Shakespeare. The texts we have today are usually mosaics made up of passages from the 'First Folio', published by business associates years after the bard's death, and a host of bootleg editions, 'bad quartos', etc., which appeared without authorization during his lifetime. This is bad news for searchers after the Truth, but good for you, since you can claim, when challenged for misquotation or getting the story wrong, that you're using a rare prompt-book version, which "seems much more *Shakespearian*, somehow".

Although it's not known exactly what Shakespeare wrote in his plays, it's now accepted that he did actually write them. None of the traditional rivals — who include Francis Bacon, Marlowe, Sir Walter Raleigh and various shady Jesuits — are now taken seriously. If anything, the tide has turned the other way, with textual scholars seeking their idea of sensation by laying a growing number of obscure plays at Shakespeare's door.

This game can afford hours of harmless amusement, but should not be attempted by the inexperienced bluffer.

Ben Jonson (1572-1652), friend and (critical) admirer of Shakespeare, went for a less slapdash, more 'correct' style himself. The resulting tragedies are painfully dull, but the great comedies, like *Volpone, The Alchemist* and *Bartholomew Fair*, where classical rigour is combined with street slanginess, are highly effective, and you should like them.

Both Shakespeare and Jonson wrote during the 'Jacobean' period, 1603-25 (so called, oddly enough, because it was the reign of James VI & I), but Jacobean Drama usually means the works of younger writers. Jacobean Tragedy is notoriously gloomy and cynical. **John Webster**, long held to be its greatest exponent, is still 'important', but has been overtaken by the punchier, less verbose **Thomas Middleton**. Jacobean City Comedy, set in London among ordinary tradespeople, is now making a comeback. Like the tragedy, it has a nasty, cynical and thoroughly enjoyable quality. Again, the big name is Middleton, but mention **Thomas Dekker, John Marston** and **Philip Massinger**.

In 1642, the Puritans realized a longstanding ambition, closing down the theatres altogether for a lengthy interval. But in the lax, post-war era after the arrival of Charles II in 1660, the dramatists made up for lost time, writing outrageously immoral, sophisticated comedies of aristocratic sexual manners with real actresses, instead of boys in drag. With them came the first professional woman dramatist, **Aphra Behn** (see also The Novel). Successful males included **Sir George Etherege, William Wycherley, Sir John Vanbrugh** and **William Congreve,** whose last comedy *The Way of the World* appeared in 1700, just in time to qualify for this section. The rest is Theatre.

LETTERS FROM AMERICA

American literature as we know it started with the early puritan settlers, who turned out uplifting religious verse and prose by the yard, largely indistinguishable from that of their co-religionists back home. For those less concerned with the next world than with bluffing success in this, they're of little consequence in themselves, but all-important in establishing the 'Puritan Tradition' (into which, with a minimum of sophistry, you can shove just about any subsequent American writer, as member, aspirant or rebel). The one settler who *does* matter is **Anne Bradstreet** (1612-72), who knocked her male peers into a tall black hat with her powerful poetry of marriage and home life.

With the puritans sticking grimly to heavenly themes, the secular literature of the ensuing pre-revolutionary period had to wait until the mid nineteenth century to be written (see Hawthorne). The first 'important' writer of the independent America was **Washington Irving** (1783-1859), whose folksy tales like *The Legend of Sleepy Hollow* and *Rip Van Winkle* have real charm and finesse, but show the sort of fussy would-be-Englishness against which **Ralph Waldo Emerson** (1803-82) was soon to inveigh. In *The American Scholar* (1837) and elsewhere, Emerson, a leading Transcendentalist (don't bother about what it means, just say he was one), demanded a new, all-American literature — manly, strong, and free of 'European' morbidity — starting a new tradition within the puritan one: that of the writer as 'real man'. The truly 'American' writer is no bookish nancy-boy: he can chop wood and mend walls. He has knocked about, and seen a bit of life. His art is as big, broad and confident as America itself. He doesn't whinge at ladies in their soirées, and ladies, more at home with the mincing little rhymes of the Europeans, find his work too 'strong'. Many American writers sat up at this call to arms, but found themselves unable to deliver. A tide of protectionism and schizophrenia followed, with 'serious' writers busily purging their work of imported 'Europeanisms', while praying desperately for favourable responses from Europe and, indeed, from the US bookbuying public, who remained unmoved by Emerson's strictures.

Edgar Allan Poe (1809-49) ignored his patriotic duty completely. Drawing shamelessly upon the most decadent Europeans available, Poe's literary activities — his gothic tales and verse, his sci-fi, and his novel, *The Narrative of Arthur Gordon Pym of Nantucket* (1838) — were thoroughly un - 'American'. The classic mid-century novelists, **Nathaniel Hawthorne** (1804-64) and **Herman Melville** (1819-91), also dodged the Emersonian draft. Straight out of the original puritan tradition, their sense of sin was too highly developed for a really 'confident' outlook. Hawthorne sidestepped the Brave New World issue, setting much of his most radical, morally searching work (including *The Scarlet Letter*, 1850) in colonial times, before the new nation had been born. In his *Moby-Dick*, 1851 (*the* 'Great American Novel') and in most of his other works, Melville takes his complex preoccupations — moral, psychological and literary — to sea, outside US territorial waters. Emerson had more luck with **Henry David Thoreau** (1817-62), who determined to become a 'real man' himself, by building a cabin on Emerson's land at Walden Pond, and living 'self-sufficiently' for two years. As his later account of the experience, *Walden* (1854) reveals, he was a fine prose stylist but a ludicrously incompetetent backwoodsman, helped through by regular supplies of Mom's home cooking and constant support from friends. Thoreau, ever dismissive of such 'detail', judged the experiment a complete success — as, unaccountably, has his American posterity.

Emerson really hit the jackpot, though, with **Walt Whitman** (1819-92), whose hectoring verses, singing the praises of America and the American poet, sprawl jubilantly across the page, scorning effete props like rhyme or fixed metre, piling up images in incantatory lists. Whitman wrote one mighty work, *Leaves of Grass* (1855-91), which grew, as the years went on and he added ever more poems, to enormous proportions. The 1865 *Memories of President Lincoln* section, including the famous elegy *When Lilacs Last in the Dooryard Bloom'd*, is uncharacteristically subdued. Much more typical is the earlier *Song of Myself* (1855) where, as the title suggests, Whitman scrutinizes himself (at quite indecent length) — unlike the 'European' introspective, however, he's thoroughly pleased with what he sees. Whitman's uninhibited scope, manly energy and indisputable 'Americanness' soon got his self-appointment as National Bard ratified by general consensus, and he's been breathing down the necks of American poets ever since.

The 'American' novelist came later, with Samuel Langhorne Clemens, or **Mark Twain** (1835-1910), Mississippi pilot, roving reporter and (failed) businessman. And, of course, author of classic travel writings and novels, notably *The Adventures of Huckleberry Finn* (1855). Twain is a more convincing 'real man' than Whitman: he's so unselfconscious in his love of the Great Outdoors and his rejection of 'Sivilization', with its social graces, home comforts and tyrannizing women. If he hasn't had the stranglehold on the novel that Whitman has on poetry, it's largely because of **Henry James** (1843-1916), confirmed anglophile (and, ultimately, British citizen) who dealt in subtly nuanced, highly intellectual portrayals of American and European social manners, and the "interaction between the two cultures". The Early James of, for example, *The Europeans* (1878) and *The Portrait of a Lady* (1881), the Middle James (*The Bostonians*, 1886, *The Tragic Muse*, 1890) and the Late James of *The Ambassadors* (1903) and *The Golden Bowl* (1904) are differentiated chiefly by an increasing tortuousness in what was always a pretty elaborate style. As decadent as Poe, James couldn't be dismissed as a crank in quite the same way, and he's been a strong influence in later American literature.

Three important (and belatedly recognized) women writers burned their fingers on the 'manly' tradition meanwhile. **Emily Dickinson** (1830-86) kept her undeniably idiosyncratic and 'incorrect' — but extremely original and powerful — verses of psychological and spiritual crisis to herself after an early batch came back from a distinguished critic covered with red ink. Her poems were published in stages after her death, but were much too 'unhealthy' for her century. **Kate Chopin** (1851-1904) wrote 'Frenchified' stories about the Creoles, Cajuns and other undesirables of the South. Her great novel, *The Awakening* (1899), took a less than enthusiastic view of marriage, and that wasn't well-received either. **Edith Wharton** (1862-1937) had more success, but only as a Jamesian disciple — a role which, with patronizing encouragement from the Master, she all too readily accepted. As *The House of Mirth* (1905) and *The Age of Innocence* (1920) show, she couldn't pile up the subordinate clauses quite like James, but she has a greater social range, more incisiveness and, predictably, a "better understanding of women".

Twentieth-century poetry got off to a reasonably 'healthy' start with **Robert Frost** (1874-1963), whose poems extol the wholesome, hard-working country life.

Frost was un-Whitmanesque in his restrained, traditional 'English' verse-forms, his tendency towards self-doubt and thoughtfulness in poems like *After Apple-Picking* and *Desert Places* and his viciously pessimistic streak (see the 'nasty accident' poems — boys killed by chain-saws etc.). His heart was in the right place, though, and with his more overtly political forties and fifties poems of (WASP) American destiny — notably the insufficiently controversial *The Gift Outright*, 1942 — Frost assured himself Whitman's mantle of 'American Poet'.

If this garment sat a little uneasily on Frost's shoulders, it was a better fit than it could have been on any of his early contemporaries — a thoroughly decadent bunch. The great corrupter was renegade mid-westerner **Ezra Pound** (1885-1972), who presided over the emigré scene in London and Paris through the second and third decades of the century. As champion of Imagist poetry, which favoured the terseness and precision of imagery of oriental (and some classical) poetry over the abstract ramblings of the 'Great' English and American poets, Pound was crucial. As Imagist practitioner, however, he is less important than **H.D.** (Hilda Doolittle, 1886-1961), **Marianne Moore** (1887-1972) or **William Carlos Williams** (1883-1963), who avoided the conspicuous erudition of the others, combining Imagist concision and exactness with homely American colloquialism, writing about wheelbarrows, cats and waste-paper rather than Ming vases and orchids. Pound quickly abandoned Imagism for Vorticism, a muddled and confusing theory — all you need to know is that it produced the muddled and confusing *Cantos* on which Pound was to work for the rest of his life. He still found time, meanwhile, to back fellow writers like T.S. Eliot — and, eventually, to give vociferous support to Fascism.

Among Pound's other finds was the **Lost Generation**,

a large, loose-knit (and loose-living) group of expatriates in Paris, sharing feelings of 'alienation' and disillusionment, enjoyment of the favourable exchange-rate, and little else. Among the most important, **Gertrude Stein** (1874-1946) attempted, with considerable success, to free language from the constraints of 'meaning', and has become a permanent figurehead for *avant-garde*-ism. **F. Scott Fitzgerald** (1896-1940) and **Ernest Hemingway** (1896-1961) both admired Stein's work, but preferred to cultivate their own styles. Fitzgerald, in novels like *The Great Gatsby* (1925), went for a rather precious aestheticism; Hemingway, in *Fiesta* (or *The Sun Also Rises*), 1926, and later works, for a studied yobbishness. Neither author thought much of life. Hemingway has been given a hard time over his undeniable *machismo*-obsession. However, with the impotent 'real man' hero of *Fiesta*, Jake Barnes, he did hit the manly American tradition right where it hurt.

Not everyone shared the pessimism of the exiles. **Hart Crane** (1899-1932), for one, tried to present a more optimistic view of the world — and of America — in *White Buildings* (1926) and in his masterpiece, the long poem *The Bridge* (1930). Built around the somewhat improbable central image of the Brooklyn Bridge, this is a brilliant, exciting, but in places frankly incomprehensible, tribute to a strong, buoyant, futuristic America. **Wallace Stevens** (1879-1955) worked on through the twenties, apparently oblivious of all the fuss abroad, at the peculiarly difficult poems he was to produce all his life. Insist that you find them "witty" and enjoyable. They rejoice in titles like *The Idea of Order at Key West, Anecdote of the Jar* and *The Emperor of Ice Cream*, and all concern "the problems of the artist in organizing and interpreting his world". (N.B. Be sure to remember that 'rage to order' does *not* mean anger on demand.)

The great new talent of the thirties was **William Faulkner** (1897-1962) who, after a false start writing virtually meritless poetry, found his vocation in 1929 (with *The Sound and the Fury*) producing extremely depressing novels and stories on the depravity of Southern life. In this and subsequent works, including *Absalom, Absalom!* (1936) and *Go Down, Moses* (1942), Faulkner brought a 'Joycean' experimentalism to what had previously been the preserve of boring realist writers. This doesn't make it any less dismal. Faulkner's work opened up the rich seam of 'people treating people like dirt in the South', mined by hosts of younger contemporaries, including two — both women — who really were good, and had new things to add: **Carson McCullers** (1917-65) and **Flannery O'Connor** (1925-64).

POST-WAR LITERATURE

The Post-War British Novel

From its early days in the eighteenth century, the status of the novel has always been a trifle dodgy. Written for a new, 'bourgeois' reading public, it depended for its success on mass-production and mass-marketing. In short, it had 'trade' written all over it — as the old, aristocratic, reading public did not fail to observe. It also sought to entertain rather than to improve or impress, so couldn't really be classed as 'literature' at all. The writers of the new form were, by and large, parvenus, with no social position to lose, and those who weren't hid behind a bewildering array of pseudonyms. Indeed, one of the main causes of modern 'Birth of the Novel' disputes is the web of evasion and obfuscation woven around their work by the authors themselves, who went to elaborate lengths to convince their readers that they were writing true-life memoirs, moral handbooks, historical accounts — anything, in fact, but 'novels'.

Much the same state of affairs prevailed through the nineteenth century, and up until the 1940s, when critic **F.R. Leavis** put the novel on the literary map as the most respectable of all forms. Creating the tastes of the succeeding two decades, Leavis asserted that the 'serious' novel could be truly great art — but (and this is the really ingenious bit) that only Austen, Eliot, James, Conrad and Lawrence had delivered the goods, and were 'mature' enough to be worth reading. 'Leavisites' had to maintain an awesomely high moral tone, but for a 'Great Tradition' with only five authors who would complain? As a bluffer you can only look back on the passing of these values with regret, and shed a bitter tear for the sneers and contumely now directed at this enlightened, misunderstood man (in so many ways the patron saint of all bluffers) — and, in public, sneer louder than anyone else. Reserve the term 'Leavisite' as a mortal insult and devastating put-down for anyone misguided enough to cross you in argument.

Since the decline of Leavisism, normality has been restored. This has had positive as well as negative results. A lot of 'classic' novelists consigned to the dustbin by Leavis have been fished out and dusted off — and you now have to pretend to know about them. On the other hand, 'The Novel' as a form is taken less seriously today, and is back in its previous position of poor relation to poetry (this despite the riff-raff who write poetry these days). As with the distinction between 'Drama' and 'Theatre', there is a simple rule of thumb: anything written before 1945 *might* be a Novel (and therefore count as 'literature'); anything written after that, whether good or bad, falls into the category of Good Read (and doesn't score as many bluffing points).

Though you won't win admiration by displaying a close familiarity with the 'contemporary' (the word is used here, as it generally is, very loosely) novel, you can't afford not to know about it. Disdain for the form is permissible; ignorance isn't. So keep quietly up to date, following the reviews, reading cover-blurbs and working out a brief 'line' on anything that seems particularly important. New novels — even respectable ones — appear in their hundreds annually, and there simply isn't time to do more than this. Reading novels is a peculiarly inefficient way of keeping up — by the time you've finished this week's masterpiece, next week's has appeared and you've missed the boat. In any case, you can be sure of finding someone who has ploughed through a given novel, and a few well-chosen questions will easily produce plot-summary, character-names, main points of interest, etc., without ever revealing your ignorance.

Novelists tend not to conform to schools or groups, preferring to write in a wilfully individualistic manner that makes life very difficult for bluffers. There are two important mini-traditions in the contemporary British novel that you should be able to spot, however. One is the 'academic' or 'campus' novel, which began in the fifties with **Kingsley Amis**' *Lucky Jim* and has been continued in the well-nigh indistinguishable works of **David Lodge** and **Malcolm Bradbury** (it is not true that they're the same person) and of **Howard Jacobson.** Light, trite and brimming with tweed-jacketed, donnish *machismo*, these novels are of very little interest in themselves. But you should know about them, as they're inordinately popular (and, indeed, the only recent fiction most literary academics have read). Then there's the less clearly defined, but more inherently interesting tradition of Austenish 'high comedy' written by — and largely about — women, which runs from **Ivy Compton-Burnett** though **Barbara Pym** to **Margaret Drabble** and her more talented sister, **A.S. Byatt**, taking in some of **Iris Murdoch** along the way (as well as male novelist **A.N. Wilson**). This tradition — aped from afar by **Anita Brookner** — is characterized by domestic setting, slow action, and characters who are too clever by half.

Most contemporary novels aren't anchored in any such obvious tradition, and are at the mercy of the fiercely competitive fiction charts, in which the top positions change week by week. The **Booker Prize** (the Crufts' of publishing) gives a broader annual perspective, though you should still criticize its "appallingly narrow range". However you mustn't ignore it, and should pretend to have read and despised the six books on the shortlist. It goes without saying that you have cogent reasons for disliking the winner even more that the other

other five ("they *always* give the prize to a man/a woman/someone with a glamorous foreign name/some ghastly right-wing traditionalist", etc.). A good line to take is "What an *outrage* that Z.Q. Smith's *Memoirs of a Harem Eunuch* wasn't nominated — such a *brave* book, don't you think?" Choose or invent your own author and title. The obscurer the better, especially if it sounds obscene. As a last resort, say you know from a personal friend of one of the judges (but you can't say which) that the whole thing was as rigged as the Cutty Sark.

The American Novel

The American post-war novel, like its British counter-part, has proved 'a rich and varied form', but its status as a bluffing subject is equally dubious. As in Britain, the novel charts in America are crowded and fast-moving. Follow the reviews, read the cover blurbs (paying closest attention, as usual, to press quotes) and, once again, allow the losers who actually take the things seriously to do the legwork. For the reasons outlined above, novel buffs don't normally get much of an audience for their preoccupations: lend a sympathetic, slightly condescending ear to their conversation (making profuse mental notes the while) and you can keep up to date and spread a little happiness at the same time.

Meanwhile, a few names to drop, so that you'll never have to go entirely naked into the conference chamber: **Saul Bellow**, **Bernard Malamud**, **Philip Roth**, **John Updike**, **Thomas Pynchon**, **John Barth**, **E.L. Docto-row**, **John Irving**, **John Cheever**, **Paul Theroux**, **Gore Vidal**, **Don DeLillo**, **Joyce Carol Oates**, **Alison Lurie**, **Alice Hoffmann** — a motley assortment from a very long list, but a start.

British Poetry

Mr Bleaney to Seamus Heaney

The first big event in British post-war poetry came in the 1950s with **The Movement**, arguably more of a standstill. Its preoccupation with toughness, hard-bitten irony and anti-pretentious plainness led in general to drably straightforward waffle in over-familiar verse-forms. Movement poets worth mentioning include **Philip Larkin, Thom Gunn, Donald Davie, John Wain** and **Kingsley Amis**. Larkin was by far the best of these, and with poems like *Church Going, Toads, Mr Bleaney* and *The Whitsun Weddings*, he assured the ascendancy of Movement values through the sixties (though his genuine ability, humour and occasional bursts of feeling would seem to place him beyond the pale).

The Movement didn't go unchallenged, though. The rise of **Ted Hughes** through the late fifties and early sixties reflected a growing feeling that poetry, far from being 'tough', had become too blandly civilized or, as **A. Alvarez**, poetling and talent-spotter-in-chief at the time put it, too 'genteel'. Gentility was never among Hughes' failings. A rogue Nature-poet, he ran amok through poem after poem about dead pigs, diabolical crows, psychopathic pike, and a vast assortment of other unpleasant fauna. The poetic public, tired of waiting for Hughes' mellower maturity, breathed a sigh of relief when, in 1984, he was appointed poet laureate and, *ex officio*, no longer a fit topic for intelligent discussion.

Hughes is now, perhaps, more interesting from an antiquarian point of view as an early influence on megastar **Seamus Heaney**. Brought up on a farm in Co. Derry,

Heaney is no stranger to the red in tooth and claw aspects of nature, and that Hughes' poems struck a chord is clear in Heaney's first collection, *Death of a Naturalist* (1966). Even at this stage, however, Heaney's menagerie includes un-Hughesian beasts, like human beings. There's also — unthinkable in Hughes — a personal (and personable) voice, which grows stronger in subsequent books. Though always strong on the facts of country life and generally being 'close to the soil', Heaney escaped categorization as rustic bullock befriending bard, exploring the more general interests — moral, religious, political and historical — of his early work. Developments in Northern Ireland were, of course, to provide an unlooked for abundance of subject matter. Heaney rose rapidly through the seventies from young hopeful to (with *Station Island*, 1985, *The Haw Lantern*, 1987 and *Seeing Things*, 1991) reigning champion. He's now so distinguished, indeed, that it's hardly worth talking about him. Sneer, if you must, at the honest-to-goodness down-home traditionalism which has endeared him to a new poetry-reading public (i.e. the middle-brows), but remember that the cognoscenti revere him too, and that you ignore him at your peril.

The Tide That Followed Seamus

A general boom in Irish (especially Ulster) poetry followed Heaney's early success. This consisted partly in archaeology, Saxon pundits realizing they'd better dig around to see if anything else had happened in the emerald isle since Yeats. It was remembered that **Louis MacNeice** (1907-63), classical scholar, translator and Audenesque poet of the thirties, and writer of the distinguished — and very readable — *Autumn Journal*

(1939), who later turned to Radio Drama (of which form he's one of the acknowledged masters), was also a native of Ireland — though living most of his life in England — and could be discussed from this angle. While MacNeice began a posthumous second career, **Patrick Kavanagh** (1905-67) was granted real importance for the first time, being the nearest thing to a proto-Heaney available. The similarities are obvious, but Kavanagh's work still seems a pale anticipation on the whole. *The Great Hunger* (1942), Kavanagh's most important work, is a beautifully written but utterly depressing account of grinding poverty, religious tyranny and sexual frustration in rural Ireland. Be warned — Hardy at his gloomiest bursts with *joie-de-vivre* by comparison.

Not all Heaney's successors were predecessors. The seventies saw a poetic outpouring from Northern Ireland that almost justified the accompanying hype. And it wasn't, by and large, ersatz Heaney either. **Derek Mahon,** a much more obviously 'intellectual' poet, bounced into the limelight with his chatty erudition and 'Augustan' wit. Mahon's verse letters, like *Beyond Howth Head* and *The Sea in Winter,* are particularly good, and his *A Disused Shed in County Wexford* a contemporary classic. More recent poems in *The Hunt By Night* (1982) and *Antarctica* (1985) show he's still turning out a quality product. **Tom Paulin** meanwhile weighed in with his first collection, *A State of Justice* in 1977. Here, and in the subsequent *The Strange Museum* (1980) and, especially, *Liberty Tree* (1983), Paulin shows a passion for politics not shared by the other Northern Ireland poets , along with a growing passion for indirectness, with today's situation 'refracted' through an assortment of odd historical moments in various far-flung countries. This development continues in Paulin's loose translation of Sophocles' *Antigone, The Riot Act* (1985). Many victims of his (all-too-direct) book reviews must be longing to read him it. **Paul Muldoon** has been going strong since 1973. Though much too young for elder statesmanship, you could claim that he's obviously going to inherit Heaney's mantle. His best early poems are anecdotes rather than confessions (less penance for the reader): recently, though, with *Immram* and *The More a Man Has the More a Man Wants*, his stories have reached disturbingly shaggy-dog lengths. *Meeting the British* (1987) has short dramatic monologues ('ventriloquism') instead, while the mad *Madoc: A Mystery* (1990) fully lives up to its subtitle, being simply incomprehensible.

Star Wars: The Martians Strike Back

The first serious threat to Irish domination of 'British' poetry came in the late seventies with the rise of the 'Martian' poets. The label refers not to place of origin — leader **Craig Raine** and younger sidekick **Christopher Reid** hail from Co. Durham and Hong Kong respectively — but to the title poem of Raine's second collection, *A Martian Sends a Postcard Home* (1979). Martian poetry follows the traditional high-school-exercise formula of looking at everyday things through the eye of an uncomprehending outsider — an outsider who doesn't know what a grocer is but knows a 'modest quattrocento Christ' when he sees one. It dated quickly (Raine has moved into civil engineering with his 1986 libretto, *The Electrification of the Soviet Union*), but England was now back in the spotlight, and a new poetry headquarters sprang up in Raine's adoptive hometown, Oxford, to rival that in Belfast.

Non-Martian staff included **Andrew Motion**, **John Fuller** and **James Fenton**. Fenton made a big splash with his sophisticated verse-travelogues of the Far East and Europe, but whether his reputation — or Fuller's — will survive their joint effort, *Partingtime Hall* (1987), an orgy of third-form humour in sub-Tom-Lehrer style, remains to be seen.

The eighties have seen the final canonization of **Geoffrey Hill**, whose career has been burning on a slow fuse since the late fifties. His difficult, grandiose poems of national myth and religious torment were gathered in a *Collected Poems* in 1985, to rapturous acclaim.

Tony Harrison, another eighties success, is a very different matter. Born in Leeds of working-class parents, his grammar school English master disapproved of his accent. Harrison has been flicking ink-pellets at Sir — and at the establishment's linguistic caste-system — ever since, championing the uneducated and inarticulate in dazzlingly sharp, erudite verse. Harrison's poems on his parents, in *The School of Eloquence* (1979) and *Continuous* (1982) show him at his best so far. The long poem *V* (1985) is patchier, but undoubtedly important.

Grab your shrimpnet and kiss-me-quick hat for seaside frolics with Jersey-born **Jeremy Reed**. Somewhat neo-Hughesian, lately going to the dogs with Baudelaire, he's been hyped by major critics as the one to watch. Probably worth an each-way bet. **Peter Reading**, a copybook Post-modernist (see Glossary) of violent imagination is worthwhile, but difficult. His recent *Ukulele Music* (1985) and *Stet* (1986) make *The Waste Land* look like *Daffodils*. Persevere.

'Alternative' Traditions

Beware of bluffing in them if you're not part of them.
It's in dubious taste — and, likely to land you in hot water.
As the oldest and most prestigious of the British literary
clubs, 'serious' poetry has been particularly unwelcom-
ing to gatecrashers of the wrong sex or race (much more
so than the Novel, for instance). It's not, after all, very
long since the Catholic Irish were admitted (after centuries of stereotyping as a 'poetic' nation).

Black West-Indian British poets now have a semi-
respectable anthology (James Berry's 1984 *News for
Babylon*) but it looks like being a long time before they're
invited into 'ours'.

Women have gained a somewhat tenuous foothold. Of
the two major agenda-setting anthologies of the past
twenty-five years, Alvarez' 1963 collection boasts two
women, out of twenty-eight poets — both American, and
one a pal's wife. Morrison and Motion's 1982 collection
does better, with five out of twenty. But in their
polemical introduction dealing with the important poetic
developments (the main *raison d'être* of such anthologies) it's clearly a man's art, and women are strictly 'any other business'. Out-Gay poetry is also barred
pretty thoroughly.

The bluffer's task is, of course, to follow literary
fashion unquestioningly (you need only appear to lead
it), and the fact that you can get by admirably in complete ignorance of anything other than the male
'mainstream' need occasion no concern for the straight
white male with his mind on bluffing *realpolitik* —
there's enough data to retain as it is. Bluffers whose sex,
sexuality or race (or, for that matter, radical aspirations)
put them at odds with this mainstream will want to look
further, to (in the first instance) Alternatives (p. 67).

American Poets

The two giants of post-war American verse are already among the dead: Okie **John Berryman** (1914-72) and Boston-patrician **Robert Lowell** (1917-77). Both started in the forties with rather derivative, academic work (though you can afford to praise, vaguely, "some of" *Berryman's Sonnets* and poems by Lowell like *The Quaker Graveyard in Nantucket*). During the fifties, each turned to increasingly direct poetry about the tortured psyche — a trend that culminated for Lowell in *Life Studies* (1959) and for Berryman in the *Dream Songs* (1964). Berryman stuck to this theme until his suicide — a professorship at Minnesota State University being, some have argued, the last straw. Lowell's sixties poems are more concerned with his own distinctively confused brand of liberal politics. With works like *Waking Early Sunday Morning* and *For the Union Dead*, Lowell did, you should say, become "one of the few *genuinely* important public poets" — but concede that they're "less taut" than his fifties output. Between them, Berryman and Lowell started the mini-tradition of agonized 'confessional' poetry, picked up in the sixties by **Sylvia Plath** (whose most important book, *Ariel*, 1965, was assembled by her widower, Ted Hughes, after her suicide in 1963) and by **Anne Sexton**, as well as by a host of vulgarizers. This sort of writing is either loved ("the only authentic kind") or hated ("It's *sick*"), and it's not easy to hedge. Try "respecting its enterprise" but "regretting its ultimate failure".

While Berryman and Lowell dominated the fifties mainstream, two important outsider groups were forming. The **Black Mountain** poets (based at the North Carolina college of that name), led by **Charles Olson** and including **Robert Creeley**, **Ed Dorn** and, more peripherally, **Denise Levertov** and **Gary Snyder**, believed (like everybody else) that verse should follow natural speech patterns, not 'distorting' metre. They cultivated the precision of Pound and William Carlos Williams, with the latter's interest in the 'ordinary things' of America. This produced — in sixties work like Snyder's *Myths and Texts*, Olson's *West*, and Dorn's *Gunslinger* — dashing, if sometimes phenomenally difficult, twists on the 'Great Outdoors' tradition. Their technical innovations are still influential.

More famous and more fun (though less 'important'), the **Beat Generation** rose on a Lost Generation-ish ticket of alienation, rootlessness and (mostly internal) exile. The traditional Beat Bible is **Jack Kerouac**'s novel *On the Road* (1957), but you can get a feel for the movement more quickly with a glance at **Allen Ginsberg**'s *Howl* (1956). A lament for oppressive, bourgeois America, *Howl* also celebrates the Beat lifestyle of drink, drugs, dosshouses and modern jazz. Stress that the Beat values of 'roughing it' and male camaraderie place them firmly in the Emersonian 'American' tradition (though perhaps not what the sage had had in mind) — more so than other modern writers, and that the flagrant homosexuality of Ginsberg in particular makes explicit what was always implied in that tradition. Ginsberg, and other Beat poets like **Gregory Corso** follow Whitman in their relaxed, sprawling, incantatory style. Recall with affection Ginsberg's imagined meeting with the great bard in *A Supermarket in California*.

During the sixties, the Beats and Black Mountain-ites were admitted to the mainstream. This was something of a defeat for the former group (for whom an *entrée* to the new bourgeois 'pop culture' was no substitute for real outsidership), but the latter gained from the security, writing much of their best, most individual works.

The 'new' up-and-coming fringe group — productive but unrecognized during the fifties — was based in New York and known, for want of any better label, as the **New York Poets**. 'Art-critic poets' would have been a more accurate, if less convenient, title, since they drew heavily upon the theories of modern painters like Jackson Pollock, Michael Goldberg and Robert Motherwell. Avoid discussion of specific contributions. The most immediately likeable of the group was **Frank O'Hara**, who loved jazz, the movies and Manhattan street-life as well as aesthetic theory, and whose great poems (like *The Day Lady Died* and *Ave Maria*), though highly sophisticated, have a special, easy-going bonhomie as a result. O'Hara died in a car crash in 1966, and has become a favourite subject for the 'What might X have become if (s)he'd lived?' conversations you'll occasionally have to participate in. What his friend, **John Ashbery**, became is one of the top mainstream poets since the War. Working at his "great poetic project of aesthetic exploration" through the sixties, and finally hitting the big-time in the mid-seventies with *Self-Portrait in a Convex Mirror,* Ashbery is now accepted as "natural successor to Wallace Stevens". Given that we have to have one, we might have done much worse — though never quite the charmer O'Hara was, Ashbery is still a readable and exciting poet.

Like Ashbery, **A.R. Ammons** had been writing for many years before he made the limelight in the seventies. A scientist who went to the bad and started writing poetry, his background outs in his work — essentially 'Nature' poetry — in bursts of scientific terminology (words poets aren't supposed to know, like 'chloroplasts', 'entropy', 'paramocoeia', etc). Ammons' short poems are spare and impersonal; he lets himself go a little more in his grander, long poems like *Sphere: The Form of a Mo-*

tion (1974), though he's never exactly 'confessional'. **Amy Clampitt**, another late discovery, published her first collection, *The Kingfisher,* in 1983, at the age of sixty-three. Clever, allusive and daring, she gives the impression of having been everywhere and read everything. However irritating, she's undoubtedly brilliant and original, and you should say so. It's not yet safe to say that her range betrays lack of depth, that her flirtations with the great European poets of the past smack of 'literary tourism', or to make any of the other snide comments that spring to mind.

Try not to look blank if someone mentions **Robert Pinsky** or **Robert Hass**. They're not really important, but a small and devoted following thinks they are, and it's as well to be prepared. Followers of Rationalist critic and poet **Yvor Winters**, last heard of in the forties railing against Romanticism *and* Modernism, they go for the severely 'analytical' style Winters attributed (with limited justification) to the English poets of the eighteenth century.

More interesting altogether is **James Dickey**, who won notoriety in the sixties with a less than tasteful poem about sex-starved farm boys called *The Sheep Child* (and yes, it does mean what you think it means). Pretty staid to start with — in technique if not in subject matter — Dickey became more 'experimental' as he got older. This trend was first marked by his 1976 book, *The Zodiac,* which launched something of a 'second career'.

Also worth keeping an eye on is **Galway Kinnell**, another sixties figure, author of the 1960 hit, *The Avenue Bearing the Initial of Christ into the New World* (economy in title-length is *not* Kinnell's forte) whose stock has been rising again lately. Refer approvingly to his *The Correspondence School Instructor Says Goodbye to his Poetry Students* — if you can remember all that.

Language and Differences

Whether or not the many distinctive usages of American English make it a language in its own right is debatable (and indeed much debated). The bluffer should take advantage of a widespread sneaking suspicion that they might do. Non-Americans are easily cowed (even by other non-Americans) when confidently told that they don't understand the "American Language" ("That reading would work well enough if X were writing in *English*"; "Yes, but we're talking about an *American* writer", etc).

More care is needed when dealing with actual Americans, who naturally think they do understand their native tongue. On the other hand, the American literary tradition makes them particularly sensitive to charges of 'Europeanism' from anyone, and you can score cheaply by hinting that their English is too – well, *English*.

ENGLISH ELSEWHERE

Australians

Despite the popular British assumption that 'Australian Literature' means the wording on the lager cans (and, at a push, the verse of **Clive James**), there's more to it than that, and Australia has produced a good many distinguished writers (especially novelists) in its comparatively short history. Its first writer of note was **Henry Handel Richardson** (actually Ethel Florence Richardson, 1870-1946), a major Naturalist (see p. 55) novelist, at her best in the trilogy *The Fortunes of Richard Mahony* (1917-29). **Christina Stead** (1902-83) wrote several very good novels. Far and away the best — and incontestably 'great' — is *The Man Who Loved Children* (1944), about a man who didn't, and who positively loathed his wife, though never bright enough to realize this.

More famous, and "perhaps more consistently good", is **Patrick White**, who's been producing one major novel after another since the thirties. Though a Nobel Prizewinner, White is "Dostoyevskyan" — and therefore good bluffing if not light reading. The 1957 *Voss* is probably still his most famous work, but you should also be aware of later novels like *Riders in the Chariot* (1961), *The Solid Mandala* (1966) and the 1979 *The Twyborn Affair*. White remains undisputed top dog in contemporary Australian fiction, his most distinguished junior, **Hal Porter**, having died in 1985 and **Thomas Keneally** providing no competition.

Australian poets have made much less impact abroad. **Peter Porter**, however, won considerable (and quite inexplicable) renown in Britain during the sixties. He's still published — and presumably someone must read it.

New Zealanders

New Zealand has a short but distinguished 'English' literary tradition. It has also managed to take on board its indigenous (Maori) traditions more successfully than Australia (whose aborigines have never found a secure place in the 'mainstream'), most obviously with the modern English-language poems of **Hone Tuwhare** and, more recently, of **Keri Hulme** (which you should prefer to her over-popular novels).

The first major fiction New Zealand produced came in the early twentieth century with the beautifully atmospheric — if somewhat depressing — stories of **Katherine Mansfield** (1888-1923). Mansfield is still New Zealand's most famous literary name, and she's cast a long shadow over subsequent fiction, though later novelists — notably **Frank Sargeson** (1903-84) — have arguably written much better. **Janet Frame** has created some rather inept poetry, but her novels, if extraordinary in style, are undoubtedly 'major'. She's probably at her best in the three volumes of her autobiography: *To the Is-land*, *An Angel At My Table* and *Envoy From Mirror City*.

New Zealand has been more consistently successful in producing internationally-respected 'English' verse. First off the mark was **Eileen Duggan** in the 1920s — ''historically significant'', even if her verse seems a little insipid now. In the thirties came the more satisfactorily heavyweight **Robin Hyde** (actually Iris Wilkinson), and the first publications of today's elder statespoets **Charles Brasch** and **Allen Curnow** (the most 'brilliant', if not the most 'important' of New Zealand's poets). The death in 1972 of **James K. Baxter** (who probably *is* New Zealand's most important poet) and defection of **Fleur Adcock** — now effectively a

'British' poet — has left these veterans ruling the roost longer than they can have anticipated.

South Africans

Apart from **Roy Campbell** (who produced some accomplished satire in the 1920s but, with his decline into a peculiarly inane form of fascism, ultimately became more famous as sick joke than as poet), South Africa has had little international success with its poetry. Its novelists have fared better since **Olive Schreiner** wrote the country's first 'classic', *The Story of an African Farm*, in 1883 — a powerful novel about racial and sexual oppression in the veldt, and a milestone in the 'feminist novel' tradition. The next classic didn't appear until 1948, with **Alan Paton**'s *Cry, The Beloved Country* — South Africa's biggest-ever international popular hit. Like all popular hits it should be disparaged — gently, though, because Paton's heart is clearly in the right place, and it's a genuinely moving novel. You should naturally prefer his less familiar *Too Late the Phalarope* (1953).

Since the sixties, top novelist has been **Nadine Gordimer**; there's a good deal to be polemical about in modern South Africa, and Gordimer has come under fire for excessive indulgence in liberal propaganda, in novels like *Occasion for Loving* (1963), *A Guest of Honour* (1970) and *Burger's Daughter* (1979). She is certainly less stylistically adventurous than fellow-liberal **J. M. Coetzee**; but whether all his experimental dabblings in Kafka make him the more successful 'artist' is less clear. His 1980 *Waiting for the Barbarians* is interesting — though "overrated": his 1983 *Life and Times of Michael K.* is rather worse — "massively overrated".

Black South Africans aren't ideally situated for making forays into *belles-lettres*. But some have struggled through, and gained a degree of international recognition, including novelists **Alex La Guma** and **Bessie Head**, and poet **Marzisi Kunene**.

Doris Lessing, born in Persia (now Iran), brought up in Rhodesia (now Zimbabwe), and a British resident for nearly forty years now, requires a mention, and it might as well be here. Essentially a politically-committed (left) Naturalist, with a strong interest in the social position and psychology of women, she's nevertheless passed through several phases: straight realism (early books, notably *The Grass is Singing*, 1950); growing experimentation and increasingly explicit feminism (from *The Golden Notebook*, 1962); radical Sci-Fi (mid-late seventies), and back to realism (eighties). The Right have never really liked her work, and each successive phase has convinced one or other section of her readership that she's 'written out' — most recently the 'Hard Left', who considered *The Good Terrorist* (1985) a sell-out, and her 1987 Afghanistan travelogue *The Wind Blows Away Our Words*, conclusive proof that she's gone over to Washington. Neither response is fair: she is a highly distinguished writer, and you should like at least *some* of her work.

Canadians

Canada is not the literary wasteland most people think — it just has "a mainstream of outsiders". Canada's important writers have belonged overwhelmingly to 'minority groups'. If not Jewish, they have been French or Feminist. **Saul Bellow** was born in Montreal, though the general critical consensus is that his best works were written after he moved down to Chicago at age nine. Montreal Jews who stayed around until riper years include novelist **Mordecai Richler**, whose best works, written during the fifties, are firmly rooted in his local and ethnic background, and **A. M. Klein** (1909-72), without much doubt the best English-language poet Canada has yet produced.

French-Canadian writers have an older (and arguably stronger) tradition behind them than their English-speaking counterparts. Since **Emile Nelligan** wrote his Symbolist poetry at the end of the nineteenth century, there has been a steady output of quality literature. Recent talents include poets like **Anne Hébert** and **Jean Guy Pilon** as well as novelists **Gabrielle Roy** and **Yves Thériault**. The least formally educated of all these, Thériault is by far the most consciously 'Canadian'.

Among the feminists, the most 'important' is **Margaret Atwood**, whose 1972 *Surfacing* made a big splash. Her 1986 *The Handmaid's Tale* is a "feminist *Nineteen Eighty-Four*". Opinion is sharply divided about this novel — if in doubt, play devil's advocate. **Joan Barfoot** is less famous, though her second novel, the murder story *Dancing in the Dark*, is now a film. Take advantage of the still-obscure first novel, *Gaining Ground* (1978) — a "feminist *Walden*" (though nothing like so dishonest).

Playwright and novelist **Robertson Davies** is something of a misfit in that he doesn't belong to any of these minorities. He made his name as a writer of witty, sophisticated comedies of Canadian manners in the early fifties. His reputation — and his technical adventurousness — have increased since then. Davies' *Deptford Trilogy* (published together in 1980), *The Rebel Angels* (1982) and *What's Bred in the Bone* put him among the top English-language novelists writing today.

GLAMOROUS FOREIGNERS

Nothing wins bluffing credits like an ability to waffle about foreign language writing, and it's much easier to do than you'd think. Much of it is available in translation (certainly enough for your purposes), though you should stress that you've read the original version, criticize the translator and use a slightly altered, stilted form of the English title (e.g., 'A Century of Solitariness', 'Ivan Denisovich's Day', etc.) so that it sounds like your own impromptu rendering. Lament the "shameful dearth of decent translations" in the "xenophobic" English-speaking world, which "keeps important work from a wider audience" (you, of course, are at the show already, in the front row).

And now, a lightning tour of top attractions in the bluffer's European empire...

France

France is as good a place as any to start — England's closest continental neighbour, it remains a place of mystery, and its writers, like its perfume or cigarettes, carry exciting overtones of elegance, sophistication and decadence throughout the Anglo-Saxon world. 'Greats' of the past start with the medieval poet **Villon** (who wrote verse while taking time off from his main occupation of pathological criminal). Renaissance writers included **Rabelais**, unparalleled master of the smutty, scatological joke (but now important as 'proto-modernist' experimenter), and poets **Du Bellay** and **Ronsard.** The seventeenth century brought the great 'neo-classical' dramatists: the comic **Molière** and trage-dians **Corneille** and (top French playwright) **Racine.**

Racine's writing is stately, eloquent and monotonous, but you can stir things up nicely by preferring him to Shakespeare. The really big names of the eighteenth century — **Voltaire**, **Diderot** and **Rousseau** — were, like many later French writers, "Philosophers first and *writers* only second". In the nineteenth century came the great Realist social novels of **Balzac**, who gave his fast-moving melodramas — arguably too readable to count as 'art' literature — a spurious respectability by calling them, collectively, the *Comédie Humaine*. Later in the century, **Flaubert** and **Zola** put on a more convincingly 'literary' showing, turning Realism into Naturalism with their precious, lovingly 'aestheticized' accounts of physical and moral squalor.

Poets discovered squalor earlier, in the mid-century, with **Baudelaire** (whose *Fleurs du Mal* should be among your favourite reads) starting the Symbolist tradition which continued through the later work of **Rimbaud** (not to be confused with his similar-sounding fellow-aesthete played by Stallone) **Verlaine** and **Mallarmé**, through to the early twentieth century, with **Valéry**. They believed, roughly, that the material world they perceived served only to symbolize an ideal, spiritual world beyond, which given the immorality and material degradation some of them cultivated, was perhaps just as well. You can still score points (with middlebrows) by describing anything involving a sudden burst of memories as "Proustian", after **Marcel Proust**'s *A la recherche du temps perdu* (1913-27), a gargantuan epic of introversion and nostalgia, and cautionary tale for those given to dunking biscuits in their tea.

In the poetry of the twenties, Symbolism gave way to Surrealism, with **André Breton** and **Apollinaire** leading the great excavation (through dreams and automatic writing) of the unconscious mind — and pretty strange it looked, too. The next important craze came in the thirties with the Existentialists (led by **Sartre, de Beauvoir** and **Camus**) who wrote novels and plays illustrating their theory that the universe was a chaotic mess in which you were on your own, that to think otherwise was 'bad faith', and that it was therefore up to you to assert your autonomy by making a deliberate 'existential choice' to commit some 'gratuitous act' (shooting an Arab was one method favoured by Camus).

Literary interest in the post-war years centred on the spectacle of Sartre moving in and out of the Communist Party until **Alain Robbe-Grillet** and **Nathalie Sarraute** caused a stir with their plotless, characterless 'anti-novels' in the sixties. Since then French writers, with the exception of the brilliantly clever but by recent French standards laughably lucid **Michel Tournier**, have made little impact in the English-speaking world. The experiments of contemporary writers such as **Hélène Cixous** in striving to produce 'unreadable' texts have proved too successful for their works to have travelled well. But though the Anglo-Saxon nations have never warmed to the compulsive intellectualism of the French, and always affected to disdain the literature that results, a residual feeling that 'they may write drivel, but they're much smarter than us' means that today's French writers, like their forebears, make ideal bluffing material.

Germany

German literature, like that of France, is regarded with dislike — but also with awed respect — by English-speakers. Once again, the offence is over-intellectualism — not the brilliant but (we hope) shallow intellectual games of the French, but an earnest, ponderous, 'teutonic' building up of immensely abstruse (but unquestionably 'serious') philosophies of life, death, history, creativity, the place of the artist in society — you name it... Fortunately, there's no need to know much about all this, since the mere mention of Germany's great Romantic poets like **Goethe**, **Schiller** and **Hölderlin** is enough to subdue most of your competition, reminding them that with Shakespeare, Milton or Jane Austen they're simply messing about with kids' stuff.

Germany has been assisted in this century by the enlistment in its literary ranks of assorted foreigners. The Czech-born **Franz Kafka**, once prized for his 'terrifying vision', is now a "comic realist". *Never* call things 'Kafkaesque'. **Rainer Maria Rilke** (a Czech-German-Austrian writing in German, Russian, French, Italian...) has a very dropable name with some fiendishly difficult mystico-metaphysical poems to it. Austrians **Robert Musil** (author of the extraordinarily long *Man Without Qualities*) and **Hermann Broch** (author of the relentlessly dull *Death of Virgil*, called by some The Novel Without Qualities — "Virgil ought to sue for libel") are useful heavyweights. Native Germans **Thomas Mann** and **Bertolt Brecht** could also throw their intellectual weight about. Mann (despite film score by Mahler) is serious, his irony crushing, his only comic novel, *Felix Krull*, uncompleted. You needn't bother with Brecht's Marxist aesthetics (enough people already have); despite attempts to alienate the audience, his *Threepenny Opera* verges on the Good Night Out. Find obscure plays or (better) prefer his poetry.

Hermann Hesse may have been an important novelist once, but his posthumous role as guru to the Hippy movement makes him an untouchable. Much better bets are post-war giants **Heinrich Böll** and **Gunther Grass**, of whom the latter is the superior writer — inventive, wide in scope and penetrating in political vision — but the former, an amiable, rather pedestrian satirist, won the Nobel Prize (winners of which you should automatically deem "overrated").

Romanian-born **Paul Celan** (1920-70) is undoubtedly post-war Germany's top poet. A holocaust survivor (his parents, like most Romanian Jews, weren't so lucky), the experience naturally influenced his poetry, which wrestles passionately with the problem of evil. Poets since his death have inevitably seemed trivial by comparison.

Italy

Greatest of the early Italians is **Dante**, whose *Divine Comedy* is still the best bluffer's guide to Hell, Purgatory and Heaven. Even if the humour appears to have dated, it's a "milestone in Western Culture" and has given Dante all-but-divine status ever since. As pioneer of the 'Sonnet Sequence' (see p. 18), **Petrarch** has a lot to answer for. Respect his "revolutionary technique", and deride middlebrow objections that his abject praises of Laura seem 'insincere' (actually the only thing that makes them bearable). **Boccaccio** is also worth a mention. His *Decameron* makes him one of the greatest ever collectors of lewd stories (and contains more names for the male member than you ever dreamed existed).

After the Renaissance, nothing likely to prove useful to the average bluffer happened until the 1950s, when **Giuseppe di Lampedusa**'s novel, *The Leopard,* was published (a few years posthumously). Hugely overrated, but unfortunately 'important', it captures all too successfully the dull, empty life of a decaying aristocracy.

Even slower than the cult film with Burt Lancaster. **Italo Calvino** started life as a straightforward, if talented, realist. But he went wild in the late fifties with *Our Ancestors* — a decidedly eccentric pedigree of cloven viscounts, non-existent knights, etc. He ended up in his last major work, *If On A Winter's Night A Traveller* (1979), writing eleven novels at once, including one of the reader reading *If On A Winter's Night A Traveller*. This may sound contrived and rather pointless, but it's what Post-Modernism is all about, and if you can't stand the pace, literary bluffing's not for you. Among what Calvino calls 'Books That Everybody's Read So It's As If You Had Read Them, Too' come the highly cerebral best-sellers of **Umberto Eco**, *The Name of the Rose* and *Foucault's Pendulum*. Feel free to 'discover' allusions to obscure writers and philosophers nobody else has spotted.

Spain

Spain "has, of course, the least *European* of European literatures". Decline to be more specific than this, but murmur something about "Arab influences in the Middle Ages". Spain's rich and distinctive literature has been neglected elsewhere which, whilst being a "scandalous omission", makes your life a lot easier.

You need to know, first of all, that Spain's sixteenth and seventeenth-century Golden Age produced **Cervantes**' *Don Quixote* — an 'immensely influential' (and long) novel, which few have actually read, as well as the great dramatists **Lope de Vega** and **Calderón de la Barca** — both priests with a shockingly unclerical taste for violence. Then, from the late nineteenth century, there's **Leopoldo Alas,** influenced by 'Naturalists'

Flaubert and Zola (see France) but recently 'discovered' in the English-speaking world as a top-flight novelist in his own right.

Apart from **García Lorca,** the great Modernist playwright and poet, and bard for the Republican government (generally thought to have been assassinated by fascists in 1936, though Allen Ginsberg claims to have spotted him in *A Supermarket in California*, in 1956) you should also know about **Valle-Inclán,** experimental novelist, poet and dramatist of the twenties. Use the word "Joycean", but bemoan its inadequacy. Literature had a thin time of it under Franco, and Spanish writers churned out little else but grindingly realistic novels of their people's sufferings. For really original work you have to go to exiles, notably novelist **Juan Goytisolo**.

Eastern Europe

Nineteenth-century Russia was a grim place, if the literature is anything to go by: **Chekhov**'s characters do nothing but whinge about cherry orchards and the price of a night out in Moscow, while **Tolstoy**, after tackling War, Peace, and Adultery with crushing seriousness, came to the staggering conclusion that his writings had been too frivolous, and went right over the top with pathologically moral tales like *The Kreutzer Sonata*.

After a promising start in graveyard humour in the style of **Gogol**, the depressive in **Dostoyevsky** came up from the underground — and Tolstoy really does look frivolous alongside his doomladen late novels. **Pushkin** (useful to know that he was one quarter black) was slightly more cheerful, despite being exiled by the Tsar for writing 'seditious' poems. **Osip Mandelstam**'s poetry also managed to get on the wrong side of the establishment — in his case, Stalin. The 'Russian Futurist' **Mayakovsky**, on the other hand, went down well not only with Uncle Joe but with the impeccably dissident **Boris Pasternak.** Since the film of his novel, *Dr Zhivago*, it's best to treat Pasternak as "a poet first and foremost". **Alexander Solzhenitsyn**, after many years of dissident celebrity, finally made it to the West, and promptly started telling Westerners where to get off. Needless to say, it's no longer OK to like him.

Other East Europeans of your acquaintance should include Czech novelists like **Jaroslav Hasek** (creator of the unwittingly subversive buffoon, *The Good Soldier Schweik*, 1923) and the more recent **Josef Skvorecky** — whose best novel remains *The Cowards*, 1958 — and **Milan Kundera**. Stress that Kundera's over-mannered, trifling novels of the last decade, which have made his reputation in the West, aren't a patch on earlier works like *The Joke* (1967). Mention also the contemporary poet **Miroslav Holub**. Poles of note include **Bruno Schulz,** whose thirties tales — fantastic, comical and brilliantly original — make him the nearest thing to a "second Kafka" there is, and a major figure in his own right. You should also be aware of contemporary novelist and film-director, **Tadeusz Konwicki,** as well as **Czeslaw Milosz**, who remains, though an exile of a quarter century's standing, Poland's most important contemporary poet (despite the infallible poetic touch of His Holiness, Pope John Paul II).

With Eastern Europe now in turmoil it is impossible to get a true picture of what is happening on the literary scene day by day. As usual, such confusion favours the enterprising bluffer, for whom great opportunities are opening up in the region. Nobody is really in a position to contradict you, whatever you choose to say.

Latin America

The never-ending quest for cheap exoticism has taken bluffers to much more distant climes in recent years. Since the late sixties, Latin America has been *El Dorado*. Those wishing to dodge the Latin-American issue completely can argue, with some justification, that 'El boom' resulted from exchange-rates that allowed US and British publishers to snap up 'cut-price classics' produced by cheap, Third World labour. They can also point out that Europeans are attracted to Latin-American literature by superficial curiosity about a mysterious continent, misread it as pure fantasy, with patronizing disregard for its seriousness, and are happy, in contrast, to remain in almost complete ignorance of Spanish literature (which they might have more chance of understanding). But Latin America is a fruitful bluffing area, and while these objections provide useful put-downs for better-informed rivals, you shouldn't take them too seriously yourself.

Poets **Pablo Neruda** and **Octavio Paz** first put Latin-American literature on the map in the twenties and thirties. Revolutionaries — political and literary — their experiences in Surrealist Paris and Civil-War Spain, as well as their strong sense of South-American identity and culture, give their poetry a stirring eloquence and a sophistication that never seems 'pseudo-European'. Neruda, a Chilean, kept the political faith until his death in 1973, soon after the CIA (apparently unmoved by his verses) had deposed his friend Allende in favour of the amiable General Pinochet. Paz, never quite as committed, hasn't been on speaking terms with his Mexican ('socialist') government since they stopped a 1968 demonstration by the simple expedient of shooting the participants, killing over 300. He has been drifting steadily to the right ever since. Even international celebrities Neruda and Paz, however, aren't a patch on Peruvian **César Vallejo** (1892-1938). Comparable to his younger contemporaries in background, European 'education' and aims, Vallejo outclassed them and is, "quite simply, one of the great poets of all time". (He has the additional bluffing virtue of being comparatively unknown). This trio has proved a difficult act to follow, and later poets have made less impact internationally. One exception is Nicaraguan priest and sometime Sandinista minister **Ernesto Cardenal,** impressive enough as a hero perhaps, but overrated as a poet.

It's fiction, not poetry, though, that has made Latin America's name recently, and the writers chiefly responsible are Argentinian **Jorge Luis Borges** (d.1986) and Colombian **Gabriel García Márquez**. Borges wrote important poetry, but he's most famous for his odd little stories — impersonal, highly erudite metaphysical puzzles. He also had odd little likings for Gaucho knife-fights and General Pinochet. Whilst you're free to disapprove of these hobbies, utmost admiration for Borges' work is mandatory. García Márquez became Latin America's most popular export in the sixties, with *One Hundred Years of Solitude, the* classic of 'Magical Realism'. An over-used term with as many definitions as practitioners, Magical Realism is a distant descendant of French Surrealism. Developed by fifties writers like Cuban **Alejo Carpentier** and Guatemalan **Miguel Asturias**, it incorporates fantasy and myth into its perceptions of 'real life' — as in practice we all do ourselves. García Márquez was first to make the technique really work, though, and *One Hundred Years of Solitude,* like his later work, makes stunning reading. Like most other important Latin-American writers, García Márquez does not share Borges' fascist sympathies (though he presumably had his fingers crossed when he vowed to publish no more work until Chile was rid of Pinochet).

Others have benefitted from the success of this pair. Argentinian **Julio Cortázar,** for one, scored a big hit with his dazzling 'Borgesian' horror stories, though his hyper-sophisticated novels won little more than raised eyebrows. Peruvian **Mario Vargas Llosa** has also made a splash with *Aunt Julia and the Scriptwriter* and *The War of the End of the World* — but neither of these recent works can compare with his 1961 *The City and the Dogs* (so it's fair to say that "He has *definitely* fallen off since his sell-out to the Right"). Disaffected Cuban **Cabrera Infante**'s *Three Trapped Tigers* may be 'Havana's *Ulysses*' but it doesn't travel well. Much too clever for his own good, Infante has written ever more impenetrably with advancing years, and is regarded with increasing scepticism. Mexican **Carlos Fuentes,** though still scribbling, has never recaptured the form he found in his novel of the Mexican revolution, *The Death of Artemio Cruz* (1962). More recent arrivals on the scene include Argentinian **Manuel Puig** (the film of his *Kiss of the Spider Woman* is, of course, "a travesty!") and the well-connected but "overrated" **Isabel Allende**.

Under the useful heading: 'Major Novelists The Boom Missed' come some of the best writers of all, including Mexican **Juan Rulfo**, of whom a rival acidly observed: 'His reputation grows with each book he doesn't publish'. He died in 1986, the long-promised *La Cordillera* still undelivered. But the one novel he *did* publish, *Pedro Páramo* (1955), was enough to put him among the greats of the century. Other 'unjustly neglecteds' include Rulfo's compatriot, **Jorge Ibargüengoita** (another "What might he not have achieved?" genius, killed in a 1984 plane crash), Argentinian **Ernesto Sábato,** and

Carlos Onetti, from Uruguay. Brazilian writers have largely been passed over *en masse*. The main exception is **Jorge Amado**, whose rollicking comic potboilers have proved popular (though the 'serious' realist novels of his early career are still ignored). Amado's many neglected betters include late-nineteenth century novelist **Machado de Assis** — a great and original writer by any standards — and more recent figures like **Joao Guimaraes Rosa** and **Raquel de Queirós** (one of Latin America's foremost women writers, and a penetrating observer of a *macho* culture).

The Rest

Few English-speaking readers venture beyond Europe and the Latin-American colonies, and the bluffer cannot normally go wrong by treating the rest of the world (i.e. most of it) as one great Antarctica.

You might still run into the odd person rash enough to have read the lunatic ravings of Japan's **Mishima** during his brief vogue some years ago, who feels that the suffering involved merits some compensation in the form of bluffing points (don't award any). Japanese culture is preferred in its diluted, English form, in the novels (not in themselves without interest) of **Kazuo Ishiguro**. 'Indonesian literature', for most English-speaking readers, still means Somerset Maugham, and 'Chinese literature' (God help it) Pearl S. Buck, the thirties American novelist and generally acknowledged winner of the hotly contested 'Most Undeserving Nobel Prizewinner Ever' title. India is rather more adequately represented by **Salman Rushdie** (though Kipling, Forster and Paul Scott have died hard).

The Middle East, being that much closer to the

'Cultural Centre', has fared better. Israel, bringing together communities who'd been producing great literature for many centuries before the brutal disruption of the holocaust, got off to a remarkably prompt start. A distinctively 'Israeli' literature has already developed, most familiar to the world at large through the novels and stories of **Amos Oz**.

The prevailing view of Arab literature combines deep respect for its ancient traditions with complete ignorance. Be aware of influential Iraqis **Nazik al-Mala'ika** (foremost modern woman poet of the Arab world) and **Badr Shakir al-Sayyab,** whose experimental verse of the fifties opened the way for later poets like Syrian *Adonis* (Ali Ahmed Sa'id) and 'Israeli' Palestinians **Mahmoud Darwish** and **Rashid Hussein.** Any familiarity, however slight, with these writers will put you ahead of the field in an area that's likely to grow in importance.

Black African literature is pretty much a closed book, and likely to remain so for the forseeable future. The English-speakers of West Africa obviously start with an advantage, though, and Nigerians in particular have had some success in winning readers abroad. **Amos Tutuola** won warm, if arguably condescending, acclaim for his lively, folksy — and cheerfully ungrammatical — *Palm Wine Drinkard.* **Gabriel Okara**, poet and novelist and **Wole Soyinka** (a good all-rounder, but prefer his drama) have more secure, if less glittering, reputations.

ALTERNATIVES

Literature is, we are told, constantly changing, as new ideas, new experiences and new talents push the 'tradition' in ever-new directions. Mainstream writers may win acclaim for their radical/groundbreaking/daring/innovative/tough/honest/committed work (or even for experimenting with 'popular forms'); but unconventional outsiders shouldn't assume from this that *their* contributions will be wanted on voyage. The literary tradition has always been good at gerrymandering its boundaries — redefining itself in a manner which, whatever the stylistic changes, maintains the old *status quo*. If Leeds' local boy, Tony Harrison, made good, and found room at the top, he had to show he knew his Aeschylus first. Suitably 'feminine' women's writing has always been received with gentlemanly politeness, albeit with a good deal of condescension. Feminist writers have, alas, proved too unsuccessful in controlling their emotional ardour to produce real 'art'. The works of black writers, if noticed at all, have been greeted in the depressing language of the personnel officer — 'imaginative', 'engagingly flamboyant', but, when all's said and done, is it really *disciplined* enough to be taken on? Homosexuals of both sexes constitute a difficult case, since they began their infiltration very early on, and a literature purged of them would look pretty thin. The literary establishment tolerantly overlooks their 'misfortunes': what counts is their *writing* — their odd sexual predilections are 'irrevelant'. Those misguided enough to consider that, on the contrary, their sexuality *is* relevant, and something to be discussed openly, have not been well received.

There have always been rebels, and in the last twenty years in particular there has been a big upswing in the fortunes of 'alternative' literature, as these and other groups have moved determinedly into publishing — both as individuals and collectives. Today such 'marginal' literatures have become (almost) respectable, and indeed, in more radical circles, essential bluffing material. Whatever your motives — genuine interest or sheer modishness — the anthologies mentioned below provide a good starting point.

Women's writing has been the biggest growth area. Apart from a growing awareness that 'classic' women writers may not have been as sweet-tempered as they've seemed, there's been a boom in avowedly feminist literature. *The Penguin Book of Women Poets* (ed. Cosman, Keefe and Weaver, 1978) provides a wide, truly international sweep, and moves historically from ancient Egypt through to the 1970s. Fleur Adcock's 1987 *Faber Book of Twentieth-Century Women's Poetry* despite the quaint, Sun-never-sets grandiosity of its title (for a book including only poets writing in English), is useful as far as it goes, as is Carol Rumens' oddly-named *Making for the Open: The Chatto Book of Post-*(sic) *Feminist Poetry, 1964-84* (1986). More radical collections of contemporary verse include *Dancing the Tightrope: New Love Poems by Women* (ed. Burford, Macrae and Paskin, Women's Press, 1987) and *No Holds Barred* (Women's Press, 1987), which contains poems sent in by fans of The Raving Beauties — some famous, most not, but all of interest. Ruth Hooley's *The Female Line: Northern Irish Women Writers* (N.I. Women's Rights Movement, 1985) is a useful anthology of verse and prose from that province. Cora Kaplan's anthology *Salt, Bitter and Good* (Paddington, 1975) and Louis Bernikow's *The World Split Open: Poets, 1552-1950* (Women's Press, 1979) both provide good historical coverage of the English and American traditions of the past.

Novels are less easily anthologized, of course, but look for the well-known feminist imprints and you can't go too far wrong. Good news for students of feminist literary history — Pandora's *Mothers of the Novel* series (designed to go with Dale Spender's dodgier book of the same name) and the *Virago Classics* series now offer reprints of works by the earliest women novelists.

Many lesbian writers are represented in the collections mentioned above. Also of interest is the substantially lesbian anthology *One Foot on the Mountain* (Only Women Press, 1979) and its exclusively lesbian and more focused (with only sixteen poets) follow-up, *Beautiful Barbarians* (1987) — both edited by Lillian Mohin. New poetry by gay men can be found in Martin Humphries' 1985 anthology, *Not Love Alone (*Gay Men's Press), while Stephen Coote's *Penguin Book of Homosexual Verse* (1983) includes poems by both men and women. The under-representation of big names in this collection is only partly the result of a desire to give the others a chance. Compilers of alternative anthologies of all kinds come up against the problem of making low budgets cover the cost of buying the rights to publish from the plutocratic executors of many modern writers who lived and died in penury. Especially in the case of gay authors, some executors refuse permission, wishing to 'protect' the deceased from the 'slur' of inclusion in 'that kind of book'. The concept of 'culture as property' is one with which the bluffer in this area will quickly become familiar.

Black American writers have been attracting attention on and off since 1845, when escaped slave **Frederick Douglass** shocked genteel Yankees with his *Narrative of the Life of Frederick Douglass, An American Slave,* written to convince the bemused Northern audiences he addressed on civil rights that, cultured and well-spoken as he was, he really had been a slave in the South. But there's been a steady flow of 'Black Classics' since **Richard Wright**'s horrifying novel of the Chicago ghetto, *Native Son*, appeared in 1940, to be followed by his equally powerful autobiography, *Black Boy*, in 1945. **Ralph Ellison** followed in 1952 with what is still his only novel, *Invisible Man* — an ambitiously complex work about a man who, as far as his society is concerned, might just as well be. 1953 brought *Go Tell It on the Mountain*, by **James Baldwin,** in whose later novels the problems of being homosexual as well as black are more explicitly dealt with. Less famous, but in some ways as important, was **Langston Hughes** (1902-67), whose poetry, from his first collection (*Weary Blues*, 1926) onwards, influenced many younger Black — and White — poets. Baldwin apart, these writers have all been neglected outside America, and even the international success of contemporary women writers — like **Alice Walker**, **Toni Morrison**, **Maya Angelou** and **Ntozake Shange** — hasn't managed to change this.

As Guptara's handy paperback bibliography, *Black British Literature* (Dangaroo Press, 1986) shows very clearly, Britain's Black tradition goes back at least as far as its American equivalent. It's never achieved anything like the same profile, though. Berry's *News For Babylon* (1984) is an important start, but it's strictly West-Indian and, many have objected, too male-dominated. The nearest thing Britain has to a widely-available 'anthology' of Black women's poetry as yet is probably the four-handed collection *A Dangerous Knowing* (Sheba, 1985), which includes works by **Barbara Burford**, **Gabriela Pearse**, **Grace Nichols** and **Jackie Kay**. See also *Ain't I a Woman: Poems by Black and White Women* (ed. Ilona Linthwaite, Virago, 1987).

CRITICAL THEORY

'Literary criticism' — in so far as it existed at all, was by and large a chatty, easy-going affair, until the present century. The first serious blow to the free-born Englishman's inalienable right to doze over his *Christmas Carol* by the fireside came in the 1930s, from the (mostly American) **New Critics,** who ruled that gossip about what a rum-un Coleridge had been, or how 'exquisite' Tennyson's verse was, would henceforth be entirely out of order. Bluffers now had to be able to discuss the 'words on the page' and, in short, work for their living.

Critical descendants of these characters live on, notably in Englishmen like **Christopher Ricks** and **John Bayley,** now, paradoxically, struggling valiantly to defend the ancient Saxon values of common-sense, decency and freedom from (sorry, 'of') thought, against the much more dangerous ideas of a whole host of highly abstruse Continentals, (before whom large swathes of American academe have already fallen). A rogues' gallery of these difficult customers is given below — you should know your enemy. It should also be pointed out, however, that many bluffers have found the rewards of collaboration considerable, and the vaguest knowledge of the new theories a passport to success.

Ferdinand de Saussure (1857-1913), a Swiss linguist, didn't publish his revolutionary ideas himself, but his students — obviously among the most attentive in history — were able to put together their lecture notes after his death to produce the *Course in General Linguistics* (1916). Saussure's theory is that language is a 'sign-system' which follows its own logic, quite independent of the 'reality' it's supposed to represent — a bit like the Highway Code — and is, indeed, along with the many other sign-systems each culture has (attached to ritual, gesture, clothing, etc.) effectively the creator of that 'reality'. This is what later came to be known as **Structuralism.** Through language, a culture maps out a reality according to its own requirements, defining just what the individual will be able to say, think and perceive — and each maps out a different one. During the sixties, there was a boom in French thinkers trying out Saussurean ideas in various ways. **Claude Lévi-Strauss** explored their possibilities in anthropology, working on the far-flung primitive cultures traditionally studied, but with very untraditional results. **Roland Barthes** did his anthropology nearer home, studying contemporary French culture — fashion, sport, TV, food and just about anything else you care to name, while psychoanalyst **Jacques Lacan** brought Saussure to bear on Freud, to show how culture ordered even that most personal of things, the subconscious. **Michel Foucault** looked back over history, tracing ideas of madness, sanity, crime, sexual normality and deviancy, through the ages, to expose 'common sense' as an instrument of repression.

Though none of the above wrote literary criticism (except Barthes, a little), the implications of their work for the discussion of literature are pretty astonishing. Once you start seeing the mind of the individual as a 'social construct', defined by its language and culture, the picture of the writer sitting down, pondering deeply, coming up with an Eternal Truth, and 'expressing' it in a poem or novel, looks a bit insecure, as does the idea that a work can 'transcend' its time and place. The literary establishments of the English-speaking countries, not wishing to see the assumptions of several lifetimes evaporate just like that, were inevitably suspicious. And suspicions were not allayed by the strong whiff of Marxism that came through in much of this work.

Marxists have always seen money as the root not only of all evil but of just about everything else besides. i.e. we don't create an economic system to go with our views of life — the system creates its own version of humankind, with the right lifestyle and assumptions ('ideology') to ensure that the really important things in life — factories and finance — can run smoothly. Works of literature, therefore, like other commodities, are products of market forces, and the ideas and values they represent reflect the 'dominant ideology' as surely as government white papers (if, in some cases, less entertainingly), whether the writer likes it or not. The connexion between Keats' *Ode to a Nightingale* and rising industrialism isn't immediately obvious to everyone, and Marxist critics always had a difficult time making such connexions stick. In the idea of 'social organization through language', Structuralism provided them with a vital 'missing link' which was explored most systematically during the seventies by **Louis Althusser**. Though most famous for having killed his wife (the story that he sawed her in half is too neatly dialectical to be true), Althusser is also important for bringing the work of the structuralists — especially that of psychoanalyst Lacan — to bear on the traditional Marxist question of ideology. Arguing that it's far more than a set of conscious 'ideas', Althusser shows that ideology saturates our lives, right through to the unconscious level and our sense of 'self.'

Specifically feminist thinkers also found the new ideas helpful. While some feminists attempted, straightforwardly enough, to 'reinstate' neglected women writers of the past, and point out the bad deal women had had in the works of male writers and critics, French Feminists like **Julia Kristeva, Luce Irigaray** and **Hélène Cixous** worked to overhaul Lacan's overhauling of Freud, and produce a new, 'non-phallocentric' theory of psychoanalysis and literature. (Many feminists, however, are now suspicious of their Lacanian sisters' credentials).

Although, from the first, Structuralism was in a state of permanent revolution, each new work finding signs of nostalgic traditionalism in the last, the most radical criticism came from **Jacques Derrida,** who took his sixties contemporaries — and founding-father Saussure — to task for failing to practise what they preached, and for remaining trapped in an unjustifiable assumption that behind every text there's an authoritative 'speaking voice' that can 'tell' us things. According to Derrida words can really only refer to other words, and texts to other texts ("intertextuality" — a useful word). Philosophical and literary texts alike work hard to convince us that they have 'meaning' — point to some 'Truth' outside themselves. They fool us most of the time, but the smart critic can spot the rhetorical tricks they use to achieve this effect — and the moments at which, in contradictions and ambiguities, they give their game away — and can thus 'deconstruct' them. Derrida's strictures made his compatriots pull their socks up and start producing their Post-Structuralist work of the seventies. But Derrida and his **Deconstruction** were followed most closely in the English-speaking world. Critics saw in his work something akin to the 'scepticism' they'd been brought up on. Furthermore, though more radical than his French contemporaries in many respects, Derrida did also insist on a concentration on 'the words on the page' which — after all that Marxist social theory — came as a breath of fresh, bracingly 'liberal' air. While no structuralist has shown as convincingly as Derrida that there's no such thing as a free thought, he still offers his followers (like the **Yale School** luminaries **Geoffrey Hartmann, J. Hillis Miller** and the late **Paul**

de Man) a theoretically respectable born-again 'New Criticism'.

Marching to different drummers in the theoretical parade are **Harold Bloom** and the **Reader-Response** critics. Bloom livened up coffee breaks in the Yale staff-room by denouncing his Deconstructionist colleagues as arid nihilists. His *The Anxiety of Influence* (1975) sees the history of literature as one of oedipal struggle, each new generation of writers trying to murder its castrating literary fathers with 'creative misreadings'. The resulting struggle is not only fun to watch but may also produce better poetry.

Altogether less bloodthirsty, the *Rezeptionsästhetik* (practise saying this in front of a mirror) developed by Germans **Hans Robert Jauss** and **Wolfgang Iser** is a highly abstract theory with its roots in something called 'Husserlian Phenomenology'. It has been popularized in the English-speaking world in the form of **Reader-Response Criticism**, as propounded by American **Stanley Fish**, who argues that readers themselves construct the texts they read. The author's poem or novel is only a series of jotted notes — readers have to fill in the gaps from their own experiences of life and literature. Good writers exploit this, forcing readers to reconsider their assumptions, a process bluffers should always resist.

If **Terry Eagleton** did not exist it would be necessary to invent him. A Marxist critic by trade, Eagleton also acts as standard-bearer and sales rep for the whole gamut of modern critical theories in Britain. As such he arouses strong feelings in literary circles, and the mention of his name can be relied upon to revive a flagging conversation. His *Literary Theory: An Introduction* (1983) is essential reading for the serious charlatan — but be sure to dismiss it contemptuously as a 'bluffer's guide'.

GLOSSARY

Text — The book/poem/play/bit of writing under discussion.

Intertextuality — Words relating to words in other books; books in general relating to each other.

Discourse — A kind of non-regional dialect used by a particular social group; the verbal equivalent of ideology; language; vocabulary.

Privilege (verb) — To put (the wrong thing) first. Privileging the wrong ideology or discourse, or, worse still, the **transcendent subject**, can get you into heavy trouble.

Transcendental subject — Formerly known as the **individual** (hereinafter referred to as the 'bourgeois individual', since it is now clear that individuality is a 'social construct' and only a bourgeois-liberal-humanist would try to convince you otherwise). Believing in the transcendental subject, like believing in fairies or Father Christmas, is not done after a certain age.

Gaps/silences in the text — Sure signs that you are talking to a fan of sixties Marxist Pierre Macherey: "Is that *really* the time?"

Signifier/signified — What Structuralists call a word and what it means. True Structuralists are rare nowadays, and your companion may only be a post-Structuralist. Test the water with the old favourite: 'I'm a Structuralist — what's your sign?' Real Structuralists get cross, post-Structuralists will manage a wry smile (Non-Structuralists say 'Capricorn — why?').

Power/desire/knowledge — Not a heavy pass, just a wandering Foucaultian. You could upset him/her by asking "Don't you find Foucault's classifications rather *normative*?", or offering to give your own history of sexuality, with slides.

Presence/absence — You are in the presence of a Derridean. Absence will make the heart grow fonder.

Mirror-stage — What most littérateurs (a narcissistic bunch) never grow out of, spending hours preening themselves before a heavy date with the Other. Alternatively, you have found the only Lacanian at the party.

Carnivalesque — High incidence in books of food, drink, sex, fun and unmentionable bodily functions. Supposed to be 'subversive'. Invented by Russian critic Bakhtin when writing about Rabelais — not to be confused, with 'Rabelaisian', which means all of the above except the bit about being subversive, and is used by liberals only.

Dialogic — What Bakhtin Did Next. Having more than one 'voice' in a text. Presumably supposed to rescue the reader from the mindbending tedium of most writers' conversation.

Gynocentric text — A book with an interesting woman in it.

Gynocritics — School of thought which claims that this is a good idea and we could do with more books like that.

Logocentrism — Hopelessly old-fashioned and misguided belief that words have a fixed meaning or centre, often held by the:

Naive reader — Reader who hasn't heard of Structuralism or its legacy. A term of abuse.

Modernism — Daring, difficult, experimental works by T.S. Eliot, Joyce or any other twentieth-century writer you admire (*not* D.H. Lawrence, please). What followed then had to be called:

Post-Modernism — Self-conscious, smart-alec (but often enjoyable) literature, dogged by modern critical theory. It is 'self-referential' — a good thing — and riddled with 'intertextuality' (see above).

Hieroglyphics — a) Mysterious signs which are difficult to 'decipher' — very exciting to Post-Modernists, especially American ones; b) anything the critic can't understand.

Hermeneutics — The 'science' of interpretation, or the art of explaining things. **Exegesis** and **explication** are the processes by which this is done, though you can also talk of **deciphering** and **decoding.**

Canon — a) All the print that's fit to read (Traditionalist). b) Device for suppressing all the print that's *really* worth reading (Radical).

Resonant — Traditionalist for 'really jolly good'.

Inscribe — Write. (It sounds better that way.)

Practical Criticism — Analysing a text through 'close reading'. Like deconstruction, it works best on a small area, ensuring that poetry once again gets more attention than the novel.

Closure — A satisfactory ending. Post-Modernism 'resists' this. So do medieval and Augustan poetry, eighteenth-century novels. And, of course, *The Bluffer's Guide to Literature.*

THE AUTHOR

Michael Kerrigan was born in Liverpool in 1959. His early triumphs culminated in his captaincy of the Blessed Sacrament general knowledge team (Walton district champions, 1969). Such a pitch of achievement was inevitably difficult to maintain, and a series of reversals brought him at length to Oxford, where the academic study of English gave him the best possible foundation for a career in intellectual dishonesty.

He has posed as a publisher in London and New York, and served a term as Bluffer in Residence at Princeton University. He now lives in Edinburgh where he is attempting, with limited success, to bluff his way as a Scotsman.

In perpetrating this book, he was aided and abetted by Caroline Gonda, Alison Hennegan and Liam Rodger, and by his brothers Peter and John. While the above are accessories before the fact, any lapses of taste, judgement or accuracy are, of course, all his own work.

THE BLUFFER'S GUIDES

Available at £1.95 and (new editions) £1.99 each

Accountancy
Advertising
Antiques
Archaeology
Ballet
Bird Watching
Bluffing
British Class
The Classics
Computers
Consultancy
Cricket
EEC
Espionage
Feminism
Finance
Fortune Telling
Golf
The Green Bluffer's Guide
Hi-Fi
Hollywood
Japan
Jazz
Journalism
Literature
Management

Marketing
Maths
Modern Art
Motoring
Music
The Occult
Opera
Paris
Philosophy
Photography
Poetry
PR
Public Speaking
Publishing
Racing
Seduction
Sex
Teaching
Television
Theatre
Top Secretaries
University
Weather Forecasting
Whisky
Wine
World Affairs

All these books are available at your local bookshop or newsagent, or can be ordered direct from the publisher. Just tick the titles you require. Prices and availability subject to change without notice.

Ravette Books Limited, 3 Glenside Estate, Star Road, Partridge Green, Horsham, West Sussex RH13 8RA.

Please send a cheque or postal order, and allow the following for postage and packing: UK 25p for one book and 10p for each additional book ordered.